APPALACHIAN HERITAGE

VOL. 46, NO. 4
FALL 2018

ESTABLISHED IN 1973

PUBLISHED QUARTERLY
by Berea College
CPO 2166
205 N. Main Street
Berea, KY, 40404

www.appalachianheritage.net

 Periodicals postage paid at Berea, Kentucky, and at additional mailing offices. ISSN# 03632318.

Electronic submissions only at www.appalachianheritage.net

Distributed by the University of North Carolina Press. Basic subscription price: $30/year for individuals, $40/year for institutions. For subscription requests and inquiries, visit the magazine's website, email uncpress_journals@unc.edu, or call 919.962.4201.

CONTENTS

EDITOR'S NOTE

JASON HOWARD

Each fall, *Appalachian Heritage* devotes a special section of the magazine to a featured author, and over the years we have celebrated some of the finest writers in the country. But this year is different. Instead of a single author, we have delved into our archives to present a collection of featured *authors*—poets who, over the years, have engaged with the natural world on the page in surprising, revelatory ways.

The natural world, of course, is one of the major themes of Appalachian literature. The beauty and harshness of the mountains; the deep sense of place provided by topography and traditions; turning to the land for a living through farming, timber and coal; the natural world versus Appalachians themselves—all these are recurring themes in creative work from and about the region.

In American literature, this realm has historically been seen and treated as a man's domain, due in part to antiquated patriarchal notions involving men's supposed dominion over forests and the wild, threatening outdoors. This idea was, of course, preposterous—a fiction seen through a machismo-smudged lens that obscured the long-standing contributions of female writers. The great Phillis Wheatley, for instance, was writing about the natural world early on, celebrating "the zephyr's wing" which "exhales the incense of the blooming spring" and a God who "draws the sable curtains of the night." Emily Dickinson famously wrote about keeping the Sabbath "With a Bobolink for a Chorister — / And an Orchard, for a Dome —" And in her mystical poem "Memory of Cape Cod," Edna St. Vincent Millay conjured "the wind in the ash" and "The mosquitoes...thick in the pine-woods"—a poem I loved as a child, one that continues to sustain me.

In their poems, Wheatley and Millay were not only engaging with the seemingly restricted space of nature as women but through other excluded identities—as a black woman, in the case of Wheatley, and as a queer woman, with Millay.

Exclusive beliefs about nature have often been deeply embedded in Appalachian culture and literature as well. But such ideas were also defied from the outset, with women like Emma Bell Miles and Effie Waller Smith claiming their space and voices in the realm of the natural world.

While curating these poems, it is to that spirit I kept returning—the notion of the natural world as a common land to which we are all invited. As I read, I listened for Millay's wind, searched for the mosquito's bite. I heard it in "the rush of sound" described in Llewellyn McKernan's "Stream" and in the "lifting, lifting" of wings in Richard Hague's "Luna Moth." I saw it embodied in Crystal Wilkinson's masterful "Terrain," in which the narrator depicts herself as "a homing blackbird destined to / always return...called back home through hymns / sung by stout black women in large hats and flowered dresses." I smelled it in the dark loam of Louise McNeill's "The Three Ferns" and in the "ground cedar and springy peat" of Marc Harshman's "Not All That Much." I felt it in the heat of the Georgia summer, conjured with humidity in doris davenport's "hog killing time." I tasted it in the flavor of onions, beans, and cornbread arrayed across the table of a queer household in Jeff Mann's "Yellow-Eye Beans."

This tribute, of course, is not intended to be a comprehensive anthology of Appalachian naturalist poets. Instead I have envisioned it—or better yet, heard it played—as a symphonic movement, a piece that can stand alone, but one that is also part of a greater whole that would include other poems and poets.

Let that music—that wind—whip around you while reading these poems. Let it carry you away, off to a mountain clearing, to a great Commons for all of us to explore and tend. ■

CUMBERLAND WATERS

I drink of waters, first and last,
Mountain primed and mineral clear,
Pure rock wherein the look is cast
Of meadow calm and upland wear,
Aspects of enduring, old fields' care.
Though streams go clouded with their past,
The source is here.

No water witched by witching prong
Has brought me up to lonesome song.
No engine flocked with haste
Clocks my slow use of force.
This has a river's downward course.
This song was spoken young,
This word spoken at the source.

ALBERT STEWART

STREAM

I sleep with both sun and moon,
am the content and cup of water,

rise and fall without the benefit
of man-made law or proclamation.

Fish swim in my veins. Ferns plot
their scandals. At dawn I smell

sweeter than a deb who stands
before a mirror and dabs all

her pulse points with verbena.
All my bright eyes open at noon.

Count them if you can while I
dance. Then I'm still but I move,

my contemplation a sky that shifts
from rose to blue to grey to velvet,

myself the dark sound of a verb
that like the Tower of Babel is

clearly heard but untranslatable,
a rush of sound that deep down

and far away winds up its steel crane
and by daybreak repaves an old road—

rich and slow as molasses—
from the interior of a continent

to the river's black cold to
the edge of the blue ocean.

LLEWELLYN McKERNAN

DARK RAIN

A morning of dark rain: four wild turkeys walk
stiff-legged at the edge of the leafless woods,
picking at the wet ground. This is early,

before bitter coffee starts to flood my veins,
sluicing into the flesh of my arms and belly.
This is before bitterness tries to take the day,

before my mother falls apart, shouting
"I don't know what to do," before my
grown children precisely point out

my failings. And before all that,
I sat in the one-room school in the country
and identified myself as an eight-year old,

shameful and amazed at what I was
doing there, wearing a faded cotton dress
with grey and purple roses on it,

and hand-me-down brown shoes.
I was about to be given a double promotion
because I could read what they gave me,

although I didn't know who Pearl Buck
might be, or why the Chinese woman squatted
in the field to give birth, or what this had

to do with me. Don't take me literally,
I learned to say in high school, and kept
saying it all along. Sometimes they wouldn't

take me at all: I suppose it was
too much trouble. For awhile,
I saw what death showed me

and said what it told me to say.
It had to happen: I couldn't stop it.
Everywhere I looked, a hand had

carved a sharp stony outline
around a tree, a flower, the living
blossoms traced in hard lines, the

intricate cold shapes like the screens of
the Taj Mahal, love turned to marble.
For awhile, everything was sharp and cold,

barbed against the touch. Death had soaked into
the landscape, dried and hardened it
with dark blood. It had finally taught

me a lesson: I couldn't go on like
I was. I couldn't go on thinking
I was the only one, that the others

were here for my presence. And
my mind reeled and fell on its knees,
my mind I had been so proud of.

IRENE McKINNEY

TERRAIN

the map of me can't be all hills and mountains even though i've been geographically rural and country all my life. the twang in my voice has moved downhill to the flat land a time or two. my taste buds have exiled themselves from fried green tomatoes and rhubarb for goats' milk and pine nuts. still i am haunted by home. i return to old ground time and again, a homing black bird destined to always return. i am plain brown bag, oak and twig, mud pies and gut wrenching gospel in the throats of old tobacco brown men. when my spine crooks even further toward my mother's i will continue to crave the bulbous twang of wild shallots, the gamey familiarity of oxtails and kraut boiling in a cast iron pot. i toe-dive in all the rivers seeking the whole of me, scout virtual african terrain trying to sift through ancestral memories, but still i'm called back home through hymns sung by stout black women in large hats and flowered dresses. i can't say the landscape of me is all honeysuckle and clover cause there have always been mines in these lily-covered valleys. you have to risk the briar bush to reach the sweet dark fruit, and ain't no country woman all church and piney woods. there is pluck and cayenne pepper. there is juke joint gyrations in the youngun-bearing girth of this belly and these supple hips. all roads lead me back across the waters of blood and breast milk, from ocean, to river, to the lake, to the creek, to branch and stream, back to the sweet rain, to the cold water in the glass i drink when i thirst to know where i belong.

CRYSTAL WILKINSON

LUNA MOTH

Come a hundred miles
across the Appalachians,
it follows some creek of scent
no wider than my hand.
On an upwind stump
miles out Cranesnest,
a female clings to barkshards,
pulsing her perfume.

Tonight,
something inside me
wants to fly,
wants to turn into the wind,
my body as light as a star,
my wings like the clavicles of ghosts,
lifting, lifting.

RICHARD HAGUE

THE MAN WHO LOVED HUMMINGBIRDS

Once I saw my father
  lift from last Fall's leaves
    below our wide picture window

a hummingbird, victim
  of reflected surfaces, the one clue
    a single feather clinging above the sill.

He cradled its body in his cupped
  hands and breathed across the fine
    iridescent chest and ruby throat.

I remembered all the times
  his hands became birdcalls, whistles,
    crow's caw from a blade of grass.

Then the bird stirred and rose
  to perch on his thumb.
    As he slowly raised his hand

the wings began to hum
  and my father's breath lifted
    and flew out across the world

JEFF DANIEL MARION

READING A BOOK IN THE WOODS

The spindly trunks of two trees
have twisted twice around each other.
This is what I see when I look up
from reading. I've read the page on the right
then turned to the left-hand page and read.
I've read the book all out of order,
beginning in the middle. Now,
by looking up, I know the book
is reading me. And there I am
in a middle chapter, whistling,
and knocking the back of my hand against
the motionless fruits of a hawthorn tree,
an action that has no consequence
unless the lifted hand and the branch
left swaying after are symbolic.
I could see it that way, but also see
how simple it is, how very little
is happening—no memory
is leaking out, no evident
signs of despair. There's sort of a dot,
dot, do at this point in the book,
and I don't think the ending offers
much more. Maybe the sun goes down
and someone whistles in the dark,
or maybe it ends with pale light
still visible above the trees
and one has been changed, and walks further
into the woods and farther than that.

MAURICE MANNING

THE THREE FERNS

Ferns in their time, tricolored three:
The green fern growing by the tree,
The black fern hardened in the vein
Of coal beneath the bulldozed plain,
The white fern silvered in the frost
Upon the window pane embossed.

White is the fern that soon will pass,
Etching of crystal on the window glass,
Only the faery forest of a dream
Melting in sunlight and the kettle's steam,
Rune of the future earthlings cannot know,
The pale phantasmagoria of the snow.

"Forget the past." Old proverbs are profound.
Deep in the ribs and canyons underground
Where, in the swamps, the Brontasaurus cried,
Where in the tropic fenlands fern brakes died,
Fell with the rotting palm trees, petrified,
Layer on layer, oceans rose and fell;
Layer on layer, as the "high-walls" tell;
The rivers cutting; mountains lift and roll,
Mountain on mountain, pressing down the coal.
Black is the fern that hardens in the soul.

Ferns of the earth—there is but one:
The green fern growing in the sun,
Fronding the woodland's light and shade,
Tracing the stone wall and the glade,
Edging the beauty of the world,
Its sturdy fiddleheads uncurled

To play the wood wind's April rhyme,
The mystic notes of green-up time:

The poor man's fern in fields of broom,
The ostrich, with its royal plume,
The sweet fern, stag horn, lady fair,
The winter fern, the maiden hair,
The fern that walks from here to there...
Across the moss rock softly goes
In pixie shoes with turned-up toes.

LOUISE McNEILL

DYING BACK

On the mountain
the standing people are dying back—
hemlock, spruce and pine
turn brown in the head.
The hardwood shrivels in new leaf.
Unnatural death
from acid greed
that takes the form of rain
and fog and cloud.

In the valley
the walking people are blank-eyed.
Elders mouth vacant thought.
Youth grow spindly, wan
from sap too drugged to rise.
Pushers drain it off—
sap is gold to them.
The walking people are dying back
as all species do
that kill their own seed.

MARILOU AWIAKTA

MY COUSIN DIGS MY FATHER'S GRAVE

Time is no obsession here.
What can be done by hand still is.
So my cousin and two deacons
broke the hard October ground
with mattocks and shovels.

That afternoon we came.
Out by the barbed wire
that kept Randy Ford's cows
from wildflowers and homemade wreaths,
the deacons leaned on their shovels,
waiting to cover a man
they had not seen in years.

My cousin waited too,
under the ragged canvas tent,
refused my mother's check
with a nod, offered a few words
and his strong, soiled hand,
its confirmation of blood,
blistered from a grave well dug.

RON RASH

YELLOW-EYE BEANS

I sort them as I was taught
(is this the way the Norns
allot destinies?) picking out
gravel, bits of dirt,
the shriveled, discolored ones
not fit to eat, fated for
the trash. Sort, rinse, soak
overnight, season with
onion, hog jowl, bacon grease.
Some more objective
observer might see in
my kitchen gestures—sorting
these yellow-eye beans, or
stringing half-runners, or
rolling out pie crust or biscuits—
my father's, and, behind those,
his mother's, yours. Hillfolk
head for beans and cornbread
when the world turns surly—
pinto, yellow-eye, October.
These were your favorite.
Simmering them, I remember you.

Nanny, what would you think
of me now, twenty years after
your death, with my bushy
grizzly-bear beard, my myriad
tattoos, my lust for chest hair,
the man I live with? My guess
would be, after a short lecture
on the Bible, a book I never

much cared about to begin with,
you'd settle down to table
with us, admiring how
handsome this home is
John's made for me. I've
learned a lot in twenty years,
and at last it would be my turn
to cook for you. I promise
you'd be proud
of how well the beans
and cornbread came out
(and if you like this meal,
y'ought to taste
my buttermilk biscuits). But
before we ate, I'd invite
you to say what grace
you wanted in this queer
and pagan home, and so you
would, words brief and deep,
Pass the chowchow
following closely on *Amen*.

JEFF MANN

hog killing time

It can get hot,
up here. Further up in the mountains, it stayed cool,
even in dog days, but not here. Maybe we ain't up
high enuf, I don't know, but we get some mean hot
weather, every year. (Well, it is Georgia, y'know.)
Yeah, and it useta could get cold, every winter; we had
a hard freeze, at least one ice storm and my water
pipes would freeze up, bad. Sometimes, wouldn't
nobody on the hill have running water. But it can still
get hot. Every summer the good Lawd send, it do get
hot. Then around October, or November, when it did
cool off, finally, the leaves change, and the air feels so
good, after summer. Then, people that had 'em, would
kill a few hogs...

> What hogs?
> What hog-killing?
> When the last time you
> know somebody on the hill
> did that? The last hog
> I saw was somebody's pet,
> went in and out the house
> just like a person, and it
> was big as any three people. What
> hogs you talking about?

Not now. But it was. When the weather
changed, got cool just about like it is today, it
would be hog-killing time. And we had some
good eating, then, cracklins, cornbread, —you
name it

doris davenport

KISSING THE RIPE TOMATOES

From New Hampshire I write home to say
I miss the tomatoes I planted then abandoned
to come here. From my shady spot between two
silver tines of birches, I imagine my tomatoes
untended, drooping on their vines.
My seven-year old neighbor sends me a message:
Tell her I will kiss the tomatoes for her,
and I want to write back again, Oh yes!
Walk into the rotting garden softly,
as when you try to surprise my sleeping cat,
or when you turn in little dances you make up
for yourself. Tuck them in among their own wet
leaves and the tatters of blue shirt I gave them.
Press your lips against their cracked, exhausted
skins and let the warmth of your breath
buffer them from frost. If they must fall,
unpicked and wasted, let them go down
as we all should, whatever our accomplishments,
touched by those who care where we are going
next and who grieve our going, kissed
by a child in our ripeness.

MAGGIE ANDERSON

NOT ALL THAT MUCH

It wasn't all that much, you might say, nothing
to write home about, just
a heavy green floor of ground cedar and springy peat
littered with reindeer moss and lichened stones,
here and there evidence of flying squirrels,
muddy punctures in the cloth of the moss,
and coyotes, their ropey, black scat,
and overhead a canopy of
birch, beech, and red spruce,
the latter the local's *yew pine* whose pointed, black lances
bristle along the ridgeline.
Not that much, perhaps, and our only companion,
a still and remembered, peculiar silence,
a silence with weight,
and the kind of karma you can't get
from books, or gurus, or poets.
I lean against the grey birch,
or sit on the white sandstone,
or kneel in the faded leaf litter, and pray
without thinking God or prayer,
pray by simply staying put, letting
time fall away from me, letting
thought fall away from me
until it's just me, and this, these
things that don't seem all that much
but are.

MARC HARSHMAN

BLUE TICK MONGREL,
PACING THE PITTSYLVANIA COUNTY LINE

This blacktop tells of possum scent
But I lead myself to a red dirt rising,
Where lanky pine trees bend
And whistle in wind.
I stop and sniff, then pace
Again, a dog intent on going somewhere.

I travel with squared haunches
Past tobacco fields all yellow
With a tawny scent and let
The bumblebee buzz me by.
Even in sleep my paws twitch
With the dream of this plateau:
I'm running to the creaking pines,
Orange with dust, padding over silent straw.

Let me be I tell the truck:
I left my shaded yard months ago.
Strange men with smokehouses
Shall not capture me though at night I bay
For hearths and table scraps I've forsaken.

I am the hound you find pacing, up
Into the curve of scarlet horizons.
My blood tells in the way I hang my head
And move a little side-ways
That I have a coyote way of knowing—

Somewhere close there's a circle
Of raccoon eyes, high
Among pines that praise the sky.

ANNIE WOODFORD

DISCOVERING I WAS AND WAS NOT ALONE

It was in a night forest
of glowing aspen and beech,

the flashing eyes of creatures
forgetting me between blinks.

Like stars, my superstitions salted
darkness with past light.

All that I did not know surrounded me,
sage embrace of the cosmos.

I had little more than intuition—
faith and *a priori* scrying:

I must slow-tumble
the field stones of ignorance.

Clouds overhead like giants looked down,
then the shallow water I stepped in

looked up at me all the way home. The river's
voice sighed syllables of everything

forgotten; algebras of understanding
thin-hid under the skins of opaque houses.

RON HOUCHIN

PARADISE REGAINED

I, who erewhile the happy Garden sang
By one man's disobedience lost, now sing
Recovered Paradise to all mankind...
—*John Milton,* Paradise Regained, Book One

When I laid down in love
and got up in shame, they sent me
to my aunt in Charleston. Hot,
ripe, and fetid, the overbearing
green pressed me into myself.

Of an evening, I learned to take
the breeze on the widow's walk,
the rolling blues of the harbor
cooled my eyes, allowed me
to stretch, unfold, breathe.

Approaching storms sent the ocean
rolling like a procession of ridges,
on and on until I believed I stood
on the mountain where my kin slept,
the wrinkled ridge and valley blue,
purpled, and frothy with dogwood.

In the rising night, the moon glittered
on the swells like a cold blue
Hunters' Moon on first frost,
dark shadows mimicked inky deep hollows.
I kept vigil until the gale drove me below.

My grippe packed, I left but
a note. The preacher will condemn,
the whispers burn and scald,
I listen only to the mountains
that called me home.

JANE HICKS

THE CARYATIDS OF APPALACHIA

Small-town, hill-farm
aunts and grandmothers
who spoke in fossils
and smiled out of faces
weathered like sandstone
the limestone drape of the dresses
stark against the trees.
They chiseled lives out of flint
and ground their bones for bread.
Now they are gone under granite;
their carven names alone remain
and every name a poem:
Agnes Emeline, Sarah Caldonia,
Lillie Fay, Rilma Glenith, Victoria Jane—
the list goes on of mountain women
who held up the sky.

ELAINE FOWLER PALENCIA

MINE IS A WIDE ESTATE

I am wealthy with earth and sky,
Heir to far boundaries of field and stream,
And scarce can keep track of so much property:
Cloud herd, dew diamond, midge and bee,
Wasp-way, wind's wisdom, and the foxfire's gleam
I am rich despite a seeming poverty.

Mine is a wide estate. It is a legal jest
These are a neighbor's hills, those a stranger's.
Who owns the water's speech, the hornet's nest,
The catbird's mew, the grassy breath in mangers,
And who in cricket song and may-fly nymphs invest?
I am possessor and possessed.

JAMES STILL

THIS IS WHERE I'D START AGAIN

JULIA HOGAN

The car my brother drowned in was my dad's first. A 1989 Chevy Celebrity, with manual windows and a special key for the ignition. It was the car my dad left Meridian in, and the one he returned with, a few years later, Mom in the passenger seat, pregnant with me.

When I was big enough to reach the pedals, Dad would take me out on the empty back roads, talk me through the winding curves and hungry darkness. Sometimes I'd drive him to the bar and sit outside in the Chevy, reading comics in the streetlight until he stumbled out.

I'd always imagined I'd inherit the car. I'd drive it up to the abandoned mill with my buddies, where we'd drink and smoke thin joints and talk about girls. I imagined I'd take my first girl in the wide backseat. After a football game a county over, on a side road hidden by scuppernong and pines. We'd smoke a cigarette on the hood after the fact, she wrapped in my long button down, me in just my T-shirt and boxers, glowing white and new in the night air.

Obviously, after Trent died, none of that happened. The police brought the Celebrity back to us. It was mangled, hard to look at, but my father left it in the yard anyhow. Wisteria grew over the fenders, and animals rooted in the torn upholstery. Kids came and stole the hubcaps and anything else shiny. I didn't know what my father did with the key, if he lost it or kept it hidden in a secret place. He used to sit out on the front steps in the evenings and drink bourbon and watch the Celebrity, like it was a TV show or a particularly good movie, like it was telling him stories. One day, after years of this, my mother decided it was time to get him up. My sister, Trinity, and I were sitting in the living room, watching a television show about aliens. My mother went out the door, letting the screen slam shut behind her. Through the window, I could see her.

"Get the fuck up, Clive," she said. My father turned to her, his eyes bleary. He didn't say anything. "Get up, and in the morning I'm calling the tow truck, and they're going to take that thing to the dump. You understand? I'm tired of it messing up our yard."

The neighbors were watching by now. They pretended that they weren't, but you could almost see their ears perking up.

Our whole street was one big jumble of run-down mail-order houses and trailers, dusty yards. Chickens pecking everywhere, scraggly oak trees holding the whole thing together. I could hear our neighbors when they fought and screwed and prayed. You knew who was gonna have the cops called on them, and you knew when. You knew who was dealing and buying, who was trying to quit drinking or smoking or cheating on their wife. You knew what everyone had for dinner. You knew when a kid was sick, or had nightmares, or made a good grade in school. So the neighbors knew about Trent, and what had happened. When my parents fought about getting rid of the car or each other, they paid attention but stayed out of the way.

My father stood, rocking on his feet. He pointed at my mother with a lit cigarette. "You don't understand," he said.

"What?" Mom asked. "What don't I understand?"

He half fell, half stumbled, down the stairs and into the dusty clay yard. My mother followed him.

"I lost a son too," she said. "You don't get to act like a child."

My father took a drag on his cigarette and spit the smoke out in her face. My mother waved it out of her eyes and looked at him with same look a dog gives you if you kick it. He sat in the dust, dropping the cigarette. My mother leaned down next to him. She took his thick arm in her hand.

"I'm just trying to help you get back on your feet," she said.

He let her help him up and into the house. Bright lights and colors flashed across the television screen. Trinity's eyes stayed focused on the television as my mother sat my father in his chair and handed him a glass of water. He wiped the sweat off his forehead. His shirt stuck in wet patches to his back and underarms, as if he'd been working in the hot sun, not just crying in the dust.

The television cut through the thick silence, but no one seemed to notice. I don't even think my little sister was keeping up with the show. Looking back on it, I admire her, and her ability to hold steady.

When my father's breath had steadied and he seemed to have relaxed into himself, I turned to him.

"Dad?" I asked.

"Pete?"

"Can we make a deal?"

My dad made a guttural sound in his throat. "What is it?"

"If I can fix up that old Celebrity and get her running, can I have her?"

My dad laughed. He shook his head slowly. I waited.

"Sure, son," he said. "If you can get that pile of junk moving again, you can do whatever you want with her."

I had just graduated high school. No college plans, just odd jobs around town over the summer. Maybe I'd go to tech school in the fall, learn mechanic work or HVAC or something like that. Come back to Meridian and work with my dad. But the idea of it felt like sinking. If I could get the Chevy running, I could get out, drive west through South Carolina and into the west beyond the Mississippi. The furthest I'd ever been away from home was to Gatlinburg, Tennessee, when I was eleven and my grandparents took us to the Great Smoky Mountains. The fog over the pines and the wild heap of the mountains made me want to run away from myself. I still carry that urge, deep in my chest, even now, decades later.

"I want it in writing," I said, not looking at my father.

"You don't need writing, son. You've got my word. A man's word is better than any damn contract, any day."

I went to the kitchen and found a yellow legal pad in my mom's junk drawer. I wrote out my father's promises to me and signed my name. My cursive looked like a fourth grader's. My father sighed, but he took the pen when I handed it to him and scrawled his own name under mine.

Then he laughed again. "Good luck, kid."

I tore the paper from the pad and folded it into a square and stuck it in my pocket. Then I got two beers from the fridge and handed one to my father. "Good luck," I said. We clinked bottles and drank together. My mother called Trinity to bed. Before she left, she leaned into my father's chest and laced her arms around him. My dad wrapped an arm around her and switched the TV show to a baseball game.

"Go to bed, Trinity," I said.

My sister glared at me, and then left the room. I could hear the balls of her feet squeaking against the floor and the timber of her voice at the other end of the house. I felt an electric buzzing at the base of my spine and finished the beer with shaking hands.

■ ■ ■

In the morning I watched YouTube videos about reconstructing cars. My dad and I always did the basic mechanic work on his truck—changing the oil, rotating the tires, replacing drive shafts or serpentine belts. He ordered the parts off of eBay or found them at a scrap yard. I'd never worked on something as old or as damaged as the Celebrity, but I figured I could learn as I went along.

My mother came into the kitchen in her housecoat, a ratty robe with frogs on it and crowns, like a fairy tale theme. Even now, years later, certain smells remind me of that robe. A butteriness, a familiar warmth. She set a pot of coffee on. "You're up early," she said, watching me.

I scrolled through a website on rebuilding old cars, for shows. "Where's Dad?" I asked.

"What are you looking at, there?"

"Car stuff."

"He's got a job today. Fixing up some old woman's porch. You want coffee?" She poured herself a cup and waved the pot at me.

I shook my head.

"You buying a car?" my mother asked me. My father hadn't told her yet, about our deal. To me, that meant he didn't think it was real.

I had a good amount of money saved up, from years of waiting tables and mowing lawns. Birthday and Christmas money, visits from a crazy uncle who liked to hand me twenty-dollar bills when he got drunk, telling me to take a girl out somewhere nice. I figured my mom had guessed as much, that I hadn't spent much of it, and was sitting on the pile of cash.

I scraped the weeds away and once I'd done that, I could better see the damage.

"Not quite," I said. "I'm fixing up the Celebrity."

I waited for her to laugh, or tell me it was too dangerous, or would never work. Instead, she nodded.

"Well good," she said. "It's time someone does something with it."

She came out to the yard with me and sat on the steps while I began clearing the kudzu and wisteria from the car. I scraped the weeds away and once I'd done that, I could better see the damage. The passenger side door was smashed and hanging on by a rivet, and two of the windows were broken. The windshield was spidered with cracks. All the tires had gone flat and seeded. But once the weeds were gone, it didn't look quite as bad. It at least looked like a car, and not a wild thing from the woods.

I popped the hood and peered into the dusty interior. The mechanics looked untouched. A little rusted, with some dead weeds sewn between parts, but not completely unrecognizable. I touched the cold metal and almost felt like crying.

When my father got home, early to beat the heat of the day, we took the truck and a list of parts and went to the junkyard to find what I could scavenge. My father rode in the passenger seat, chain smoking.

"I bought that car when I was seventeen," he said. "And it was old then. Got it from some Russian man with a thick accent. My dad went with me, to make sure I didn't get scammed. The man had an old dog, named Plumber, and when we were ready to buy he asked us if we wanted the dog, too. I almost said yes. I only half think he was joking."

My dad laughed, wheezing slightly, and ashed his cigarette in the wind. "A dog and a car. What more does a boy need?"

"A girl," I said, and my dad laughed harder.

I grinned at him. The drive to the junkyard was long and hot. The truck didn't have AC, but my father kept the window rolled down and the breeze felt better than any Freon.

"When your momma and I first started dating, I went to pick her up from her dormitory. She was still in undergraduate, for nursing. I showed up in that Celebrity and she laughed at me. She said no way was she getting in that heap of junk. She made me let her drive. The funniest part of it is that the Celebrity lasted way longer than her cheap-ass Honda. Stuff was just made better, way back when."

"Way back when, like you bought a car from the 1800s and not 1980s?" I said.

My dad dropped his butt in the ashtray. "They didn't have cars in the 1800s, jack ass."

■ ■ ■

The junkyard was filled with men who fixed up cars for a living. They'd buy scrap parts and then put them in unsuspecting customer's cars and charge them 1200 dollars for a radiator change. You paid two dollars to get in, and then five dollars a pound for anything you took out with you. No telling if a part worked or not. You just had to hope. My dad didn't offer any advice as we walked around the hot and dusty yard, side stepping men in cowboy boots and coveralls who were way more prepared than I. I'd brought my tool set, a present from my sixteenth birthday. My dad carried it and that was the only assistance he offered.

You can't find a 1989 Chevy in a junkyard anymore, but you can find enough parts for it to not matter. Anything else, I'd have to buy online. I figured I could buy a couple of different things and see what worked. As I was unscrewing the parts from a carburetor, I saw a man and a woman yelling at each other across the bed of a dented pickup truck.

"You gonna take all that, you might as well take the whole car," the woman said.

"I don't need the whole damn car. This is a scrap yard, not a grocery store. It's first come, first serve. You should know how that works."

My father looked up from his phone to watch the fight play out, as well. "What in the hell do you mean by that?" the woman asked.

The man looked down into the hood of the pickup and didn't answer.

The woman went over and pushed at him. "Talk to me. Come on. You started this. Now tell me what you mean."

"Would you get off of me, woman?" The man pushed the woman away and she stood a few feet back in the dust, sulking. He lifted whatever he wanted out of the hood and carried it toward the loading deck at the front of the yard. The woman waited a minute, before following him.

"This isn't even the right kind of car," I heard her say, before they disappeared between the rows.

My father turned to me. "Son," he said. "Get you a woman who will argue with you in the middle of a junkyard in June. Otherwise, I don't want to hear about her."

My dad was always giving me strange, specific advice about the woman I should marry. Someone who lets you cook her spaghetti. Someone who doesn't like roses. Someone with green eyes. When I finally did bring the woman I would marry over to the house, I wondered if she was the type my father expected, the type he had raised me to want. She was from a northern state and said some of her vowels weird, in a way I thought was cute at first but grew to hate when we started fighting. I never took her to a junkyard, but sometimes I made her spaghetti, and she would taste it and say the sauce was too thin, or it needed more salt. She let me love her anyway. She said she loved that I could fillet a fish with one strike.

After we'd carried all the parts to the truck bed, my father stood back and wiped sweat from his eyes. I looked around the junkyard, at the half-scavenged cars sitting with their insides bare, the hoods up and glinting in the setting sun.

"You're certainly getting creative with this," my dad said, analyzing what I'd gathered.

"Do you want to drive home?" I asked.

He took the keys and led us home against the rich red sun. I felt like a bird, starting a new journey to the same old things.

■ ■ ■

On the Internet, I found spark plugs and headlights, new wiper blades. I kept my fingers crossed, as the packages came in, that I wouldn't have to replace the transmission. The money was dwindling, and the Celebrity still looked like a dog left out in the weather. Some of the neighbors had started hanging closer to the yard. I ignored them, through June and into July, but I could feel their eyes on me as I slowly rebuilt the car. Sometimes I would replace parts, but put the new ones in wrong or backwards. Metal bit into my hands and grease coated the back of my neck and the corners of my eyes where I tried to rub sweat out of them.

I imagined driving the car into Arizona. I looked up photos of mesas and the Grand Canyon. I read about Pueblo Indians and tried to imagine living anywhere with that amount of immense, flat dryness. *What would I do, out there, in that dry country?* I asked myself. *What wouldn't I do?* The car seemed to respond, as I set another spark plug into place and dried my hands on my shirt.

Trinity stayed out of the way while I worked, but she was always in my periphery. I wondered if she felt the same tugging in her chest, if as young as she was she understood why I had to get out of here. Leave Meridian now, or be here forever. When she grew up, she went to college and moved to the city, so maybe she understood better than I thought.

When it rained in the afternoons, summer storms shattering the sky, I covered the Celebrity with a tarp and sat in the kitchen and rested my hands. When my mother got home from work, she sat down at the table across from me and I rubbed the heels of her feet.

My mother would ask how it was going. And I'd tell her, in detail, of what I'd done that day. How I took out the carburetor and replaced all the gears, or drained the fuel lines, or changed the oil and oil filters and break lines. She would nod, and smile, like she knew where this was all going.

■ ■ ■

My father was home the day I was ready to try starting the car. I'd done everything I could think to do without replacing the whole engine. I'd even found a new windshield and fixed the side door. I went into the house, where my father was on the computer.

"Where are the keys?" I asked.

"The what?" he asked.

"For the Celebrity," I said.

He stared at me and then nodded, got up, and went to his bedroom. He pulled a shoebox off the top shelf of his closet and took out the keys—one to unlock and a special key for the ignition.

He pulled a shoebox off the top shelf of his closet and took out the keys—one to unlock and a special key for the ignition.

"I haven't taken these out since the police brought them back," he said. He held them. He wasn't looking at me.

"Why do you think Trent took the car?" I asked.

My brother had been twelve when he drowned. It wasn't a story I told. Even years later, I never mentioned my brother. My wife always felt that I should "talk about it," but some things are better left scabbed over. My brother was big for his age. He stole the keys to the Celebrity and went out joyriding during the first great flood. I never saw him again.

When I did tell my wife this story, months after we'd first met, the first thing she said was "You can't even get your permit till you're like, fourteen, right?" But that wasn't the point. That wasn't how things worked in Meridian. You learned to drive when your parents taught you. It wasn't unusual to see a four-year old on a tractor, an adult pushing the pedals, the kid steering.

Trent took the car out, even though he knew it was too low to drive in the flood. Who knows where he was going. A bridge collapsed, and the car sank. The truck might have made it. I think Trent was born with that feeling like you've got to run away from yourself. Driving helps, swerving back roads, endless distance. Maybe he figured that one out too soon.

My father handed me the keys. "Let's get her started," he said.

We went out into the yard, Trinity following. I got in the driver's side of the car and sat there for a minute, taking in the moldy air. The neighbors were gathering, at the periphery, to see if this would all work out.

I put the key in the ignition. My fingers were shaking so badly I could barely turn it. The car sputtered, coughed, but it wouldn't rev. I called to my dad. "She needs a jump."

We got out the cables and pulled the truck around. My father hooked the cables to the battery in the Celebrity. He revved his truck until the Celebrity caught. Together, we got her running. I felt the engine jumping under the hood and I started laughing. I could hear Trinity applauding and yelling from the steps. I looked up and saw my father's face in the truck across from me. He was smiling. I turned off the car and disconnected the cables. He met me in the middle.

"Well," he said. "You did some damn good mechanic work here, son. And I have to say, I'm a little surprised that after three years you could get her going again. But then, maybe something's watching out for this old car." He moved to clap me on the back but then pulled me into a hug, tight and warm. I could smell his shampoo and his cigarettes and the musty scent of sweat.

"It'll be okay, Dad," I said, but I didn't really know why.

■ ■ ■

I wish I could say I drove out of Meridian and never turned back, found myself in the wide starry deserts of Utah and Nevada, made it to the Pacific, to see the crest of ocean in front of me, the only real border I had. A few weeks after I'd fixed up the Celebrity and taken care of the smaller things, my mother kissed me goodbye and gave me many instructions on self care, and my father told me the last bit of advice he could think of, and Trinity made me a goodbye card with colored pencils and dinosaur stickers and cried a lot. Then I got into the Celebrity and started driving west.

I got as far as Spartanburg, pulled over in a gas station parking lot, and sat for a long time. I watched people get out of their cars and pump their gas under the cold light. I watched the men smoking under the awning of the station. I watched a woman crowding her children into the automatic doors and between the aisles of candy and chips. After a while, I got out of the car and bought a pack of cigarettes and a lighter. Sitting on the curb, I looked at the Celebrity, its rusted fenders and dingy white paint. The passenger door didn't match the rest of the car.

I spent the night in a dingy College Inn. In the morning, I found the number of a man who bought vintage cars and sold him the Celebrity at a loss and bought a bus ticket home. Coming back felt like settling into myself. It was almost September, and soon the floods would start again. I'd help my mother patch the leaks in the ceiling. I'd drive the truck through the streets and pick up stranded travelers. I'd watch the waters rise and feel myself sinking with my hometown, until the day the rains would dry. ■

LETTERS TO THE ASYLUM

1.

August 17, 1960

Dear Sir:

The fall rages on with no regard for grieving mothers.
We are lonesome on this hill without her. Everybody cries.
Soon we'll have blood red leaves scattered across the pastures.

Regarding my daughter, how is she getting along?
It's so hot the dogs' tongues wag out of their thirsty mouths.
The creek bed lays dry as a bone. Please tell me if you

think we should visit. Just piddled two hours in the beans,
winter'll be here before we know it. Everything dead, gone.
Don't want to upset her in any way. Would very much like

to talk to her doctor about her recovery. Her daddy
sulks through the field to feed the cows. I want to bring her
more clothes. Please, at once, let me know how she is doing.

Yours truly,
Christine Wilkinson

2.

September 22

Dear Doctor,
I would like to know how my daughter's getting along.
She seemed to be doing nicely last weekend—smiled, talked.
There come a preacher, Thursday last, to pray for Dorsie.

It's cutting season down here on the creek, her daddy's
out in the tobacco, hanging his fears on that post.

Each time I visit my daughter she wants to come home.
How much longer, please, will it be? I worry so much.
Do you think she will be able to hold out at work?

When I ain't pacing the floor, I'm piecing on a quilt.
Mondays, I day-work a bit for a woman teacher,
Keeps money in my apron pocket, my hands busy.

You think she will be able to come home on a trial?
If you do not wish to write me, please leave information.
I'll check at the front desk when I arrive on Sunday.

I kindly appreciate what you've done for her. She's
making plans for the future. My heart goes out to all.

Sincerely,
Christine Wilkinson

3.

October 17, 1960

Dear Doctor,

Regarding my daughter, I visit her quite often
but I don't seem to get to see you. Would you tell me

how she is getting along? She still wants to come home.
There is something special about early October,

Garden's coming to a close, the air is dry and crisp.
Seems like every living thing has a new coat to wear.

We got pumpkins orange as sunup down here. Silas's out
threshing cane. We'll be making sorghum before too long.

I'll bring y'all some if that's alright. We would like Dorsie
here for Christmas or she'll be struck with disappointment.

Her sister in Danville said she would come talk with you
but in case she hasn't, please let me know what you think.

I urge Dorsie to be nice each time I visit her.
Of course she is spoiled to death. I hope she's lots better.

Yours truly,
Christine Wilkinson

CRYSTAL WILKINSON

EXPLICATING BLUEFIELD

If you sound the body's deepest riddles,
map its secret paths from eyelash to thigh,
and leave with a longing that can only be
described as Bluefield, Virginia in April
when the air still tingles with the memory
of December and the hemlocks
stand frosted and silent at sunrise,
then flesh is no longer the jailer
that confines you, for ecstasy
reveals itself in all the hidden remnants
and moments, in ditch water reflections,
in the unrelenting crow combing the alleys
and parks for the brilliance bound
in bottle caps and chewing gum foil,
in all the light might hold.

RICK MULKEY

AN *APPALACHIAN HERITAGE* INTERVIEW

SALLY RUBIN

Hillbilly, the new documentary film directed by Sally Rubin and Ashley York, is an examination of images and stereotypes about Appalachia and its people. The film works to combat stereotypes of Appalachia as a homogenous region, using the 2016 presidential election as a window for examining how the region is portrayed in the national media. In the film, Rubin and York work to contextualize and humanize Appalachians, showing images that contrast with the often abused depictions of whiteness and poverty that have pervaded the national consciousness about the region. Rubin and York hope to challenge such prevailing, narrow views of Appalachia and the people who live here, prodding those with a limited understanding of the region and its history to pause and think before making jabs about class and otherness.

The film debuted on the film festival circuit over the summer, winning the Documentary Award from the LA Film Festival and the Special Award for Documentary Filmmaking from the Traverse City Film Festival, and being mentioned as a "significant Oscar contender" in the Best Documentary Feature category.

But in an honor that perhaps even surpassed these accolades, *hillbilly* received the endorsement of Appalachian icon Dolly Parton. "I'm happy to see somebody trying to cover us as we really are and not what some people think we are," she said. "It's wonderful, the attention (the movie) paid to so many areas that are so important to all of us. I'm proud to have been mentioned in the film a time or two."

hillbilly is now showing in select cities nationwide. Following a recent screening of the film at Berea College in September 2018, co-director Sally Rubin spoke to *Appalachian Heritage* about some of the trials and successes she and York had in making the film, developing an on-screen balance during the polarization of the 2016 presidential election, and providing a diverse perspective of an often simplified and stereotyped region.

■ ■ ■

Sally Rubin

EMILY MASTERS: What was the most challenging part of the documentary process when you were making *hillbilly*?

SALLY RUBIN: We had a couple of major challenges with the production of *hillbilly*. I think in some ways the breadth of the ideas in the film is certainly a strength; the film ranges wide in its coverage of psychological and sociological humanities themes that are complex and highly compelling, such as notions of regionalism, othering, code switching, co-option, stereotyping, and more. Simultaneously, the film deals with the 2016 presidential election and [includes] scenes with co-director Ashley York and her family. But this broad, sweeping look at the history of various cultural elements of the Appalachian region, including the region's reliance on coal, as well as the survey of media representations of the region over the last century-and-a-half, combined with all of the content described above, sometimes felt like more than we could really chew while producing the movie. We tried to do so much with this film. I hope we succeeded—I think we did—but it made production overwhelming and difficult at times, and long. It took four-a-half years to make this movie. And there were times when even I, as the film's co-director, had a hard time describing what this film was about.

Another major challenge with the production of *hillbilly* was working all of the threads described above into one cohesive movie. The film evolved substantially over time, as American society, politics, and culture evolved, and we had to work hard to keep up. When we began researching this film back in the fall of 2013 we were primarily aiming to make a film about the history and evolution of the "hillbilly" stereotype over the past century and a half. But as we got into making that movie, it became clear that if we were going to tell a story about what Appalachia *isn't*, we also had to include what Appalachia *is*. At that point we began to work in the alternate Appalachian identities that we so rarely see in the media— self-described "Fabulachians," "Appalachicanos," the Affrilachian Poets, and the wonderful, brave, progressive youth at the Appalachian Media Institute [AMI] at Appalshop.

In mid-2016 J.D. Vance's *Hillbilly Elegy* hit bookstores, putting the word and notion of "hillbilly" into the forefront of America's zeitgeist. And then in early 2016, with the presidential campaign in full swing, we realized we might have to work in the election. By that fall we were nearly done filming, yet we had no narrative "glue" for the film to hold its many ideas and characters together. We decided to insert Ashley and members of her family into the film, as we saw that a microcosm existed in part of her family of what was going on across the country—people finding themselves on opposite sides of the political and cultural aisle from those they love most. Weaving those four disparate threads together effectively into one movie was a huge challenge.

EM: Historically, as you work to show in *hillbilly*, Appalachian people have been exploited by media representations. Often, this stereotypical representation leads people from the region to be wary and distrustful of media and film. Did you face any opposition while you were filming in Appalachia?

SR: I would say that this was actually one of the easier areas of *hillbilly*'s production. We certainly had to gain people's trust—but any filmmaker has to do that, regardless of topic or content. I've been making films in the Appalachian region for twenty years, having begun my work there associate producing David Sutherland's *Country Boys*, filmed in eastern Kentucky, when I was twenty-one years old. That film [was] broadcast

"*hillbilly* brings new color to the Appalachian community"

—LA Film Festival

nationally on [PBS's] *Frontline* and was seen and appreciated by many folks from Appalachia. I then made my own film in eastern Kentucky, *Deep Down* (co-directed by Jen Gilomen), which was about mountaintop removal coal mining and gave me a much deeper understanding of the region.

We filmed in the region off and on for three years and worked with many of the folks who appear in *hillbilly*, including Chad Berry, Silas House, Jason Howard, Lora Smith, and others. When we launched production on *hillbilly*, our first step was to reach out to many of the folks in the region that I had worked with on *Deep Down*. Those people knew me, knew my work, and trusted that if nothing else I would bring a level of integrity to a film made in Appalachia. So that helped quite a bit with access, having those previous relationships in place and the endorsements from folks like Chad and Silas who are so respected across the region.

Silas came on as our executive producer and that really helped, plus we very early on added as project advisors many of the most well-respected and trusted Appalachian Studies scholars, such as Barbara Ellen Smith, Emily Satterwhite, Anna Creadick, Meredith McCarroll, Jerry Williamson, Tony Harkins, Kirk Hazen, and also Chad, Silas, and Lora.

EM: The two of you work hard to include diverse voices from Appalachia to combat images of the stereotypical Appalachian. How did you determine who you would feature in the film?

SR: We cast a very wide net with this. We knew we were looking for folks who were doing groundbreaking and innovative cultural work in the region, people like [Affrilachian poets] Frank X Walker and Crystal Good. We came across people all the time that we wanted in the movie, including those who ended up in the movie and many who did not.

But circling back to the diverse voices who were ultimately featured in the movie: one defining factor for who we filmed with and who made the final cut really had to do with the scenes we were able to film. When we found someone who we felt offered something new to the film, we tried to figure out a way to include them in a verite scene rather than simply in an interview. Many of the diverse voices in the movie are featured that way, in a scene actually unfolding rather than talking to camera, and it makes them easier to connect with and more compelling. Along with Crystal and Frank, we filmed with [queer singer-songwriter] Sam Gleaves and friends, Kate Fowler and her crew at AMI, Crystal Wilkinson and [singer-songwriter] Amythyst Kiah and [poet and scholar] Sam Cole, and so many more amazing people doing very important cultural work in the region. Executive producer Silas House was the one who led us to many of these subjects—his assistance in that realm was critical.

EM: Tensions run high in the footage about the 2016 presidential election. How did you balance the two sides represented in the film? Was it difficult to avoid division?

SR: There were several ways we were able to accomplish this. Almost all of the funding for the film came from government grants, both national and state. We received funding from the National Endowment for the Humanities and the National Endowment for the Arts, as well as grants from the humanities councils of Kentucky, South Carolina, Virginia, West Virginia, and Ohio. So while we never gave up any creative control of the film, there was definitely a certain subtle mandate to make a film that would respect the bipartisan views of all

Americans, rather than taking just one side. We also grappled in the editing room—a lot—with how partisan to make the film. I believe a film is more effective if it doesn't take a side, if it asks questions rather than gives answers, if it gets you to think and understand something in a new way. I was very committed to making a movie that didn't just skewer Donald Trump—plenty of other left-wing media was already doing that. I wanted to make a movie that opened up [an] understanding of a population that so few folks from urban and coastal America know about, and that meant balancing the sides represented in the film. So it wasn't easy, but it was necessary.

EM: At the end of the film, viewers are left to make up their own minds about the outcome of the election. What feeling are you hoping to leave your viewers with? What do you most want them to take from *hillbilly*?

SR: It depends on the viewer. I want Appalachian folks to see themselves in these stories, to feel proud of the way they're represented in the film, to feel like as filmmakers we have honored their stories and accurately represented the impact of the negative media representations on their lives and sense of selves. I want Appalachian folks who watch the film to feel proud of who they are and where they're from, to feel seen and validated and heard. For viewers from urban areas or areas outside the region, and especially left-wing viewers, I want them to have a new understanding of the Appalachian region. I want their vision of the region to be more complex, more three-dimensional. I want those viewers to be aware of their own complicity in generating and being entertained by those hurtful stereotypes and representations. I want those viewers to learn the impact of those stereotypes, and to think twice now about making a class-based or regional-based slur or joke. I want left-wing audiences to understand the very real, huge, negative political impact of putting Appalachian folks down, negating them time and time again. And I want *all* viewers, regardless of region or class or political belief, to learn to listen with compassion to people who feel differently than they do.

EM: Your juxtaposition of media stereotypes of Appalachia alongside people who are working to create a more complex representation of the region is a powerful one. What do you think is the power of art in shifting national misconceptions and generalizations about Appalachian people?

SR: I think it depends what kind of art you're talking about. There's art that comes from the region, such as the films the young students are producing at AMI. Those young folks are learning how to be creative, how to find their voice, and how to tell their *own* stories—something so critical, it seems to me, if we are going to focus on changing outside perceptions of the region. Then there's the art that comes from outside the region, such as *hillbilly*, which was produced by folks who have Appalachian connections and roots but are living in Los Angeles. I think and hope that our film can change people's views, can show the diversity of the alternate, lesser known and more rarely seen Appalachian identities. And I think having Ashley's story in the film personalizes the film in a way that really resonates for many Americans. The concepts and ideas in the movie become personal. The inclusion of her story brings the ideas in the film from the level of intellect to the level of the heart. It makes the film very impactful for people.

EM: A major conversation right now is how to give Appalachian people a voice to tell their own stories. You do this in *hillbilly,* and you also show how places like Appalshop are providing narrative spaces for young people in the region. What do you think is the best way to convince the next generation to stay in Appalachia?

SR: Lord, this is a big question, and a difficult one. Programs like AMI are offering young people a chance to create and be heard and to make a difference—without having to leave. We need more programs like that, more that work to uplift young folks from within. People like Lora Smith are doing all sorts of innovative work in the region working with food and farming, promoting the richness of Appalachian culture and encouraging young people to really reclaim it—and to stay. Musicians like Sam Gleaves and Amythyst Kiah are embracing Appalachian music and then "queering" it in their own way, creating traditional music with their own flair. Gifted speakers and writers like Silas House are hugely instrumental in instilling regional pride into young people through their writings and their art, and this gets young folks to stay, certainly. I've also heard about the STAY [Stay Together Appalachian Youth] Project, which sounds like it's doing amazing regional work getting young folks to stay [and] to reinvest in their communities. ■

BIG LICK: A LITANY

... for the Roanoke valley
where mountains hold the breath
of the dead between them and lift
from each morning a fresh bandage of mist.
—Carolyn Forché, "Endurance"

My daddy once smoked like the 611 steam
engine & ducked a cig out on my hand

where the sear was the size of a dime
I got the scar on my trigger finger

to point & prove I'm his daughter
when granddaddy told me this is the way

Grays mark their sons he said only
God knew why I was born wrong

bodied so I shaved my head
in the skinning shed the day after

he went off the rails & wandered
drunk down by the tracks & never

came back in time for supper
he suffered like a penny flipped

& flattened near the ties where I learned
a thing or two about mean streaks &

my summer teeth—*some are here*
& some are there—that grew

into my gravel speech : *son*
of a bitch : I am engendered

I am backwoods queer hiding
out high on Hustler in a deer

stand youth of single-wide
trailer trash where bus stop

boys spit dip & threw Mountain
Dew cans at the back of my head

& picked knife fights to cut
my stomach wide for lunch

money as a measurement of means
a gut wrench at survival a fat

chance in hell their daddies came
home with enough steam

from the rail yard to light
their asses up with the brass end

of a belt they would rather take
it out on their wives choking

women into love & other cruel
acts is how I learned to hate

the men who touched without
asking who showed up pissed &

pissed off gripping my arm
too hard a lesson in : *do as I say*

not as I do : until my skin bruised
& I overcame the scent of butter

& shame as my eyes traced
the tree line that enclosed

the valley & made the mountains
blue as my body before I found

a place more fitting for passing
through than settling in more fit

for transit than stasis to welcome
where my wounds lie white with salt.

BRANDIE GRAY

TOMBOY

I haven't spoken to my father in over ten years,
but if he's alive, I know the bottle is beside him.
His sister called after I graduated high school.
Your father has been trying to find you for a while,
she said. It's easy to forget you were forgotten,
when you don't want to be found. If I met him again,
I would pull the trigger, the misfire the sound
of my childhood in reverse. His tomboy daughter
built a home within herself and grew to love only women,
because they know how to knock before they enter.
He can only be in this poem—if I let him. I've been saving
my own life. I came out, knuckles swinging.

BRANDIE GRAY

BLACK RIBBONS

KELLY A. DORGAN

The youngest of three generations of women, my friend Ann lived with her mom and grandma on a sprawling rural homestead. The property itself served as testimony, a structural reminder of the Appalachian kinship-ways disappearing in our community. The long-dead patriarch's home loomed at the center of their land, decaying, abandoned, and flanked by two smaller homes. We waged our Dungeons & Dragons campaigns during the 1980s in one of those smaller homes, a two-story clapboard farmhouse with creaky wooden floorboards and mysterious nooks and crannies. We'd tuck ourselves away at the top of a steep staircase in a long, narrow bedroom, a kind of birth canal for our pubescent dreams and fantasies to enter the world.

Ann's family property snuggled up to the Blue Ridge Parkway, a scenic highway stretching some 400 miles through the mountains and plateaus of North Carolina and Virginia. The parkway offers drivers jaw-dropping views of time-worn ranges, rocky peaks impaling the sky, lichen-covered boulders, and plunging waterfalls. Summers brighten the roadside with the pinks and purples of phlox and chicory. In autumn, the rolling ridgelines are a heady mix of scarlet maple, golden poplars, orange sassafras, and green conifers.

Then, there's winter. Storms swoop in, drizzling ice until backroads transform into satin ribbons, black and slick. During the day, mountains shimmer with frost, but as the sun slips behind the swollen terrain, temperatures fall, and lingering wet patches ice over on shaded pavement. By night, if there's no cloud-cover, sparkling stars appear overhead like diamonds spilling across a jeweler's ebony velvet display pad. The world muffles, transforming the parkway into an intoxicatingly beautiful place, enticing to behold and indifferent to human life.

Out there, in the silence and solitude, it's easy for chilled drivers to crank up the heat, enveloping themselves in a delicious cone of warmth. It's easy to be lulled—just a bit, only for a moment.

■ ■ ■

Sitting in the backseat, I'd sulked, mentally reprimanding Ann's grandma for her sluggish driving. She was the kind of woman who'd disregarded speed-limit signs, resolutely going even slower. Back then, she had made me crazy, but she'd also been my ride to my weekend D&D sessions with Ann and Steve.

That night, the parkway was a deep-dark, the color of a decaying plum. No city lights, no streetlights, no illumination, nothing but our headlights. Our car crept, the dipping temperatures leaving the road riddled with patches of black ice, making the drive to the farm house dangerous. To me, time elongated, a sensation magnified by the parkway's otherworldliness: temperate forests, a diverse mix of deciduous and coniferous trees, rendered by nighttime into eerily simplistic shapes, no more than charcoal lines against the pitch-dark sky; behind us, the desolate road lit by bloody rear lights.

That night, the parkway was a deep-dark, the color of a decaying plum.

Suddenly, around a bend, came flashing. Hazard lights, and a car stopped in the middle of the road, bisecting the snaking strip of pavement. A man waved, a rhythmic insistence. Ann's grandma rolled to a stop.

Less than five feet tall, I had to shift and wiggle, struggling to see around the silhouetted figures of those in the front seat. Finally, peering through the windshield, I got a glimpse of a man, coatless—an oddity given the winter landscape.

All passengers climbed out, me included, planting out feet on the frozen parkway.

Only then did I see her.

Her acorn-colored hair remained strangely tidy, smooth and flowing, even though she had been cast to the roadside. She was small, my height, but unlike me her body was slight, almost elven—like the female D&D characters I favored playing.

Without thinking, I crouched beside her, reaching for her cheek and finding it cold, rubbery to the touch. Her face took on a porcelain luster in the headlights, her skin unblemished, unmarked—details that would haunt me decades later.

A young man stood over her, over me. His body, tall in stature, shrank. His shoulders sagged, and he looked to be collapsing from the inside-out. He was the fiancé, *her* fiancé: I learned that at some point, but I don't remember exactly when. Later—days, weeks, maybe months (I never recall precise measures of time related to this night)—I heard he had tried committing suicide. That would happen in the future, however. On this night, he stood, a vigilant guard with unfocused eyes and drooped shoulders.

At times, my friend Steve stood beside the fiancé, at times by me. Mostly, he faded into the background, drifting in and out of my attention, in and out of my recollections. Ann's grandma drove off to get help, taking Ann with her (I think). Like Steve, Ann faded that night, as did the man who'd waved us down. In my memory, I was left alone with the fiancé—and her, the one I would know only as the roadside girl.

My back ached, and my thighs cramped as I squatted by her. Somehow, I came to learn that she had been struck by a car. I would have to wait to hear the rest of her story, my teenage brain preoccupied, vomiting up lessons and warnings from my first aid training.

Violent trauma. Possible neck, spinal injury. Don't tilt the head. Could kill. Could paralyze.

Tentatively, I took her jaw in my hands. I lifted it forward, hoping to open her airway, wishing I could revive her with the cold mountain air. I wanted to cover her mouth with mine, to breathe myself into her, but I was terrified of doing more damage. Instead, I pulled out my just-in-case lighter—the kind that every good mountaineer carries when on a winter backroad. Thumb to the lighter's ribbed wheel, I flicked it, the sharp metallic edges biting into my ungloved skin. A warm stream of fire erupted, blue at the base, morning-sun yellow at the top, brightening her face. In her stillness, she looked to have simply fallen asleep at the road's edge.

Before my lighter flame flickered out, I saw her billowing exhalation, warm breath fogged by the cold. Deep down, however, I knew what I'd seen had been a trick: my fabricated vision the child of Hope and Desperation.

Her fiancé waited for an ambulance. I let him wait. I let him be a moment more without the burden of my newly gained knowledge:

Cradled by the wilderness, the young, supine woman would never rise again, never take another breath.

As we waited together, the fiancé spoke softly, his voice little more than the pitter-pattering of frozen rain on dry leaves. Standing vigil over the cold, tiny body of his beloved, he mumbled a disconnected story of love and hope.

College students at the local university, the couple had been looking forward to graduation, and their lives after that. They had gotten engaged recently and had been preparing to marry after earning their undergraduate degrees. That night, he had been driving on the parkway, she at his side, when they'd hit black ice. Their car had spun, careening off the road, fortunately, stopping on a slope. Really, the couple had been fortunate in so many ways. Somehow, the car had gotten snagged, just over the road's shoulder, instead of plummeting down one of the many steep drop-offs or vanishing into one of the thick rhododendron groves along the parkway; those groves have hidden crashed cars, shielding dying drivers from rescue. But their car had stopped roadside. Fortunately.

Shaken but uninjured, they had climbed out and began the long walk back to civilization.

As the fiancé sputtered out his story, I stared up at him, and I imagined: how relieved the young couple must have been when they had spotted approaching headlights. Just as they made their way to safety, an off-duty officer headed in their direction, driving on a road, slick and dark as black satin ribbon.

After the impact, one that had slung a young woman dozens of feet, the off-duty officer had parked his car in the middle of the parkway. He had flipped on his hazards, and waved down an oncoming vehicle, one that contained a grandmother and three teens on their way to play a fantasy game and hoping that their characters didn't die.

■ ■ ■

I continued playing D&D for years after that incident on the parkway. The characters I created remained the same: elven females with cascading hair and remarkable strength, and they all died—but they all returned to life too. Eventually, I left role-playing games behind altogether. I lost track of Ann and Steve, and I have no idea how they would tell this story or if that night remains coiling-uncoiling inside them.

I lost my gleaming dreams of magic on the side of a frozen road; once I'd encountered death—real death—there would be no undoing what had been done. Unlike in my role-playing games, there would be no potion to heal the heart of the off-duty officer who hit black ice at the exact moment a young couple made their way to safety. There would be no scroll or amulet to reverse the fiancé's agonizing loss. And there would be no spell to resurrect a young woman struck down early in her life.

To this day, I refer to the three strangers as: the off-duty officer, fiancé, and roadside girl.

They have names. I wish I knew those names.

They have stories. I wish I knew those too.

For over three decades I have carried these three strangers with me. I have blended a batch of vibrant, swirling images, then frozen them into a tragic, beautiful, and haunting mess. Privately, I have rehearsed my story, telling and retelling the happenings, and I have fallen in love again and again with the off-duty officer, fiancé, and roadside girl.

Here, I have made small verbal offerings about their lives and have woven these offerings into a tale of death and loss. But it's also a love story of sorts, one helping recover those who have been lost, one helping to resurrect, if only in the telling. ■

I COME TO THE GARDEN ALONE

So sweet the birds hush their singing . . .
Through the voice of woe . . .
—from the hymn "In the Garden," C. Austin Miles, 1912

He walked the hill
to the fence, fell
as he reached with pliers
to mend the break.

The deer had done this,
voracious, and his garden
done this, to him, and
his obsession to fix, to do,
had done this, too.

And now this, a single, slick stone
underfoot: simple,
unlucky, and no surprise
to anyone but him; still,
he needed no one, needed only
to be himself, alone, where he could deny
the years, believe against
the mounting evidence of the body.

There were already leaves,
the crescent yellow cherry leaves,
falling, burying him as if
he wished them to . . . , to do this.
He could have lain long.

Chance grows less lenient
with years, he knows, and so
allows them all, even the doc
room to pronounce and cherish
cause and effect, to preach and console,
while he plans another
ascent to the garden, another
raid on the inevitable, that last butternut
squash, that last glimpse of nurture, that last breath
of what takes him where he needs to go.

MARC HARSHMAN

PRAXIS

The soil is blackened with years of the north farm's manure.
Speckled green lifts from the unseen
        white flecks of lettuce
        seed sown weeks earlier.
Faith. Hope. Charity.
The large words of religion
        tangle with this mundane mix
        of sunshine and cow shit, rain,
        and the discipline
        to do, and wait.

MARC HARSHMAN

THE ELK

GARY THOMAS SMITH

In the low light of the gloaming he felt the pulse of the late evening in the cutting wind. It broke around the branches and tree trunks as it slid down the mountainside into the valley where he found himself standing, his knees aching. The waning sun surrendered ever more the violet, the harsher reds and oranges ebbing. The mountains closed and crowded him, and the valley darkened much earlier in the evening than the sky above it, which reflected the sun's light long after it had passed from view. As he'd grown older, Estill claimed to his wife that he could feel the turn of the Earth and that it knocked him off his feet sometimes. She said it was vertigo or that he was just getting long in the tooth. But her face was not in his thoughts now, and he tried to place himself in the valley where he stood. The mountains moved around him, toward him, suffocating the valley. The rushing of the creek grew nearer, and as the sky darkened, an elk burst from the weeds against the mountainside. Its enormous pale antlers tore at the kudzu vines that spanned the gap from the brushy ground to the tall, wavering trees.

Standing in front of the elk, he felt small. Its breath frosted in the air, though the mountains were green and the air warm. When it turned its head in profile the antlers weren't aimed as they should have been. They pointed forward.

It leapt into the sky and treaded across the violet rimmed in gold. Each step with its skinny hooves sent ripples across the clouds as if they were the surface of a lake. The elk rode the streaks of light into the distance as the wind picked up and the trees overcame him.

When Estill woke he still felt the chill air from the ceiling fan rushing around him. The elk was not a strange dream for him, but the antlers were different. Since he'd retired he found it harder to sleep. The doctor said his body had been used to the labor, the routine, and he'd have to find new ways to exercise during the day that were less strenuous than the mines he'd crawled through during his youth, that he'd managed as he aged, that he'd been forced to retire from before layoffs.

Early light shined through the blinds and fell on Amy's face, but she didn't move. It had crept up on him, but she was much older now. They both were. He still thought of the young her, the one with the hint of crow's feet holding Richard on his first birthday. The damp sheets were cold under his fingertips and the image of the elk came back, clear in his mind. In his youth he'd only heard tell of such a thing. For most of his life elks had been gone from the mountains, but they'd been set back into the wild in the past few years, same as black bears. They were creatures that needed a lot of territory—too big to handle people encroaching on their land. Folks spotted them everywhere once they were reintroduced, but he didn't. Every day the mines miles behind their house blasted at 4:15 p.m. on the dot. Animals were sensitive to such things. He longed for the wails of the mountain lions his father warned him about, though he never actually heard them as far as he could remember. Just the memory of his imagination, of his father's stories, was enough. His father had been gone close to forty years. When he got older their existence was more myth than a memory.

For the first time since he was a very young man he thought of Brenda, the girl he met in elementary school and would go on to date through most of high school. He felt guilty with his wife asleep next to him, but he could no more control his mind than he could the seasons. He'd not seen or thought of Brenda since he graduated—since he'd met Amy. When they were young, Brenda's dad came to their third grade homeroom for show and tell. He brought in a rack of elk antlers, which were rare then. The children all sat on the floor as he carried them around. They were smooth like varnished wood, but at their base they were dark brown and deeply grooved. The tips drew to a point and faded to a white-yellow, the color of bone or stained teeth. They'd asked how he'd hunted down the elk and were disappointed to hear he'd found the antlers at the back of their garden near the mountain. Elk shed their antlers seasonally he told them. Every year they lose them at the start of spring, and then they begin growing them all over again.

The kids took turns rubbing the antlers and, with help, they lifted them to feel their weight. Estill's hands were too small to wrap around them then, and the tallest point loomed over him. After they'd all taken their turns his teacher asked the students to get out their paper and pencils to draw an elk. Estill imagined them to look almost the same as the deer his father would bring home from his weekend trips, but the chest had to be heavier with a strong neck to hold those impressive antlers. He drew the points of the rack forward, lunging out over the snout to fend off whatever may come.

Their teacher walked around class with the natural history textbook to show them pictures of Kentucky's native elk. They'd been prominent before the population grew and people thinned them out. The teacher stopped at his desk and put the

Out of bed, Estill's morning coffee did nothing more to pull him from the dream or those memories.

book by his drawing. In the black and white photograph the elk's head was lifted to the sky, antlers branching up and out behind it, protecting its neck and shoulders. The antlers didn't sprout forward as he'd drawn them. She told him the drawing was a good effort and complimented his work but reminded him that he could ask for help if he needed it. He wondered why something so big should have to be scared of anything, why the antlers came back the way they did, why they shed them after so short a time.

Out of bed, Estill's morning coffee did nothing more to pull him from the dream or those memories. Coffee was a decades old habit, a fortifying ritual before going deep into the mountains for work. In retirement he had nowhere to be but still couldn't do without it. The smell of the beans after he'd run them through the grinder, the whistle of the kettle, and the shimmer of steam in the morning light made him feel at home. They were rites he'd never set to make or considered dropping. He always woke before his wife but never set an alarm. He liked to sit on the back porch with his coffee and listen to the mourning doves. The breeze carried the sweet smell of dew. Soon the sun would rise high enough to steal it away. Retirement had not suited him, but his body grew into it. His muscles ached less, despite his age, and the definition from years of labor faded without use.

The cordless phone on the table beside him vibrated. He picked it up on the second ring.

"What do you say, old man?" his son said.

"Beautiful morning, but I'm beat," Estill said. "Dreamed about elks again."

"Ought to talk to the doctor about your sleep."

"Well," Estill said. "What's new?"

"Nothing to speak of," his son said. "You seen any real elk your way?"

"Nary a one," Estill said. "Not in person at least."

"Guy at work was talking about them coming down from the mountains near the head of the holler he lives on. Stomping up his yard and all that."

"That right?"

"I ain't ever seen one in person," Richard said. "Stopped by the feed store and bought a salt lick this morning. The kind they keep for deer."

"If a cop sees it they'll fine you for trying to poach," Estill said.

"Nobody's going to fine me," Richard said. "I just wanted to see an elk. Ain't going to hurt them or anything, and the lick's back up in the holler. No one will see it."

"I can't blame you," Estill said. He sipped his coffee and listened to the cicada cries winding up over the mountain. It was going to be a hot day. "I'd like to see one myself."

"Guy at work said they usually come of the morning, so I figured I might catch sight of one when I come home from my shift."

"Let me know how it goes," Estill said.

"I will. Tell Mom I love her and I'll call back some night before I go to work."

"She'll be wanting you for dinner."

Richard said he would try and hung up to get some rest. He usually called in the morning a couple times a week to catch his father up on the mine. Richard worked a late shift and got in a few hours after dawn. Dark is dark when you're that deep, Estill told him. He was glad his son still had a job but worried the time would come when the mountains would give their last. Then everyone would be hurting. He'd seen the signs of it before he left. Miners and their families had been raised and fed on coal's profit, but it had left its mark on the land. In time trees would reclaim the land, and the creeks would fill with crawdads and minnows again, but people would file out on the narrow highways that snaked through the valleys. There'd be nothing for them anymore.

Estill did well in school and thought about college but decided against it. He never planned on a career in the mines, but it was hard to pass up as a young man. It was good money. He fell in love with Amy soon after high school, and they were married within the year. She'd always wanted to stay where they'd both grown up, and it never occurred to him to leave. He always thought he'd have work.

Estill and Amy didn't see their son much anymore. He'd come by some evenings when he had more than a day off at a time. He needed those days to readjust to the sun.

Richard never said it, but the late shift wore on him and so did the stress of keeping the job. You take the job they give you, he said. Richard was still a young man, but he was no longer in his twenties. He hadn't married, and after a while Amy stopped bugging him about it. If it happened it would happen—no use in making him feel bad about it.

The screen door opened and Amy joined Estill on the porch.

"You're up early," he said.

"You were a bit restless last night."

"Rough dreams."

"Talk about them?" she said. Flour stuck in the creases of her wrinkled hands that wrapped around the mug. She'd already put biscuits in the oven.

"I love you," he said.

"Love you," she said. "That Richard?"

"Sorry if he woke you. I always try to answer early as I can."

"I was fixing to be up before long anyway," she said. "Have to be down at the library soon."

"Food drive?"

"I'm helping set up." She blew on her coffee.

"Richard said he'd be over for dinner sometime. Said he'd call you."

"If he don't call me more often there won't be any dinner when he shows up."

"Don't be too hard on him."

She winked at Estill and went inside. He thought he'd see more of her when he retired, but she had her own life. His retirement didn't mean she'd be home more, so he had to learn to be alone. The timer on the oven sounded and he heard Amy pull out the old blackened skillet she used for breakfast. It was stained from years of use and seasoning. He wondered if she'd given one of their iron skillets to Richard so he'd cook more often and eat out less. Estill stood and stretched his back before stepping into the yard. The mountains were in full growth. The paths were probably covered. He'd not hiked them in years. The kudzu swayed in the wind and he waited, but the vines settled back into place. The glare of the elk's black eye had faded in his mind since he woke. He went inside to eat.

■ ■ ■

Midsummer passed and the dreams stayed. Over the warm months he'd slept less at night and started napping throughout the day. Amy never said anything about it. She kept busy and still spent most of her days at the library or volunteering for the church. She started leaving breakfast on the counter for him—cold scrambled eggs, biscuits in the skillet, gravy that had thickened as it cooled. Every night he followed her to bed and she'd fall asleep soon after he shut off the light. The only sounds in the house were the hum of the refrigerator and the click of the air conditioner. Restless nights were spent dreaming of violet skies and endless forested mountains. On many days lunch would be his first meal. Sometimes Richard's phone call would wake him. He slept when he would have been gardening, or reading, or working in the shed.

Estill woke to the sound of the neighbor's lawnmower. He squinted at the reflection of the sun on the tin roof of his shed and felt lost. He hoped he'd not slept outside overnight. Amy would be worried. The last of his coffee sat cold in the mug on the table, and he was in jeans and a shirt, not pajamas. He'd been awake earlier. The smell of gasoline and the droning of the engine reminded him of work he should have been doing. He was losing time. His underarms were damp, and he went inside to shave and clean up.

He stood before the mirror and was disoriented looking at himself. It was like the mirror had shifted down on the wall. The tool box for small repairs was in the utility room, and he sat it on the sink to check the frame of the mirror in case it was loose. He couldn't forgive himself if it fell and hurt someone. The screws on the frame were tight when he fitted the screwdriver into them. The measuring tape was new, and he slid it to the ceiling with ease to measure the distance between the ceiling and the top of the mirror, then he felt silly because he'd no idea what the distance was before—no frame of reference to compare. He put the measuring tape and screwdriver back into the tool box and snapped the lid shut. The reflection he studied as he stood with the tool box on the sink was the same as he remembered, though he knew well how he'd changed in time. His hair had thinned. His waist had expanded more than he'd admit so his jeans cut into him. His chest had lost its firmness. He wore his reading glasses most of the time now. But he seemed taller.

He stared back at himself from a different point in the mirror and felt uneasy in his stomach. He looked down to where his gut pushed against his shirt and noticed his shoes and the tread marks they'd left on the floor mat. He'd forgotten to take off his shoes. Estill threw cool water on his face. The shoes had made him look taller. Nothing was wrong with the mirror. Amy had long ago made it a habit for him to take his shoes off before coming inside. He'd been caught tracking mud around the house after she'd swept, so she broke him of it. It was strange that so small a detail could make such a difference.

Estill sat back in his chair on the porch and checked the phone. Richard didn't call as often as before. He'd been given fewer shifts at work. The lay of the land had changed. People were moving away from the mountains and mines were running at a loss until they shut down. New regulations made it harder to turn a profit, and there was little left to mine anyway. He told his son that was just the way of things, to ebb and flow, and that it would pick up again soon. There were always down times, even when Estill was still under ground.

"There's always whisperings about layoffs," Richard had said. "Never can tell if it's because of other mines going out or if it's because we're in trouble, but I'm worried, Dad."

"It'll be okay, son," he'd told him, but Estill didn't know.

The dream of the elk had not changed much over the summer. Sometimes he and the elk just stared at each other until he woke and other times he knew it was just beyond the trees. So he waited.

Estill left his chair and walked toward the mountain. He moved along the edge of the yard where the grass grew wild into the trees. His legs were stiff, but the exercise loosened them. He kept going toward the small creek that ran down through the valley where two mountains met. It separated his property from his neighbor's. He walked against the flow of the creek into the tall grass. The weeds were patchier under the trees, which took most of the sun, and the incline wasn't too steep if he stayed near the creek, so he kept going. By noon he'd moved beyond the place where he could hear the humming power lines and his neighbor's lawnmower.

Sometimes he and the elk just stared at each other until he woke and other times he knew it was just beyond the trees...

The creek pooled and was surrounded by large, smooth rocks. He sat to catch his breath and splashed water on the back of his neck and on his cheeks. A sharp white point grew out from beside the rock he sat on. It stood out against the gray creek bed. The antler was shattered at the ends where points had grown out, like twigs snapped from a larger branch. The elk could have broken it in a fight or against the rocks as it tried to shed the antler. There was just one. It was heavier than he expected, even with most of the points missing. The rounded spot where it had joined with the animal's head was rough, but the short point near the end was smooth. It stuck out like the handle of a cane. He used it to steady himself as he hiked forward, but he still saw no tracks or other signs of the elk as the afternoon passed. Amy would be home soon. He'd left the door unlocked and no note. The hike back down was much easier. Estill leaned the broken antler against a tree before he made it to the weeds and his backyard. He didn't want Amy to worry. He'd find it there the next day when he went looking for the elk again.

■ ■ ■

The hikes helped with his sleep, but some nights he couldn't stand staring at the ceiling. He'd sit on the back porch and let his eyes adjust to the way the stars lit up the mountains. They were large in the dark, a void of trees looming at the edge of the valley. The security light on the telephone pole made it harder to see the stars, but he thought of driving the dirt roads on summer nights on his way to the mines, the way the stars shined, the depth of that darkness, and the multitudes of purple that made up the pure night sky. The moon broke in through the dark trees, his car moving in and out of its light with each limb that hung overhead, as the road wound up the mountain. The lights around the mine muted the stars the closer he came, and the scarred, pale earth stood in stark contrast to the green that surrounded it. It felt like a dirty secret they hid up there—the way they tore up and bored into the earth.

By the end of summer he was waking earlier. The weeds eventually wore down into a trail that led to the pool where he'd found the antler. From there, he tried new directions. The elk would probably stay close to the water. He only went into the mountains after Amy had left for the day. His reflection had grown slimmer. He'd moved beyond the last notch in his belt. Estill took the hammer and screwdriver from his tool box and unthreaded his belt from its loops. He aimed the sharp point of the screwdriver just below the worn hole and brought the hammer down twice. It punched through the soft leather with more ease than he'd expected, but it went through to the coffee table as well. He moved a placemat over the gash in the table. The light wood beneath the varnish stood out. He was home more often than her now, so he could do the dusting. Amy wouldn't notice.

In the passing of time he'd come to wake in want—dreams of his youth, friends and loved ones lost, time passed, routines broken. It was a tiredness he carried with him through the day and into the night as he settled for bed only to rise early, unrested again. He took the elk antler with him on every hike into the mountains. The short point he'd used as a handle grew glassy and dark from the oil and sweat of his hands, and the tip of his cane was stained green from tearing at weeds and digging into the ground for grip.

From the pool, he kept following the creek deeper into the mountains. He walked so far that he didn't come across any other trails he'd made over the summer. New ridges sprouted from both sides that he didn't recognize. It was much rockier, though the trees were still thick. In the soft earth by the creek were deep impressions, and cloven hoof prints led up the mountain, so he followed. The grass grew taller and the tracks were difficult to see, but he kept moving. The mountain steepened and he stopped to catch his breath. He'd not gone so far from home before. The days had grown shorter, and Amy would be home cooking because their son was coming over for dinner. Before Estill turned back, he saw it. In the weeds sat a mound that didn't belong. It looked like a cluster of berries made from earth. He recognized the droppings, but how he knew escaped him. He climbed on.

At the top of the ridge he looked down into another valley he'd never seen. It had been cleared many years before, trees cut down, earth moved, but it was abandoned. Scars from old roads and machinery were visible even through the tall grass and saplings. It was no mine he'd ever known, but now it had been reclaimed by the mountain. The fading light cast down from over the ridge, and it was in that ebb of light, that falling away of the day when the sky purpled and the mountains darkened, that he saw the elk standing at the edge of the tree line. Its black eyes stayed on him, and the elk's leathery nostrils flared as Estill slowly stepped toward it. Deep brown fur covered its head and neck. Long muscles flexed beneath the tan fur of its body. Estill kept taking small steps, careful not to scare it away. He cast his cane aside and the elk turned in profile, lifting its head to the sky, and the great antlers cut into the light, aiming forward. ■

OUR MEN

come into the world a little too hot to trot
spun up, tossing down the milk bottle, fists
curled in the crib, my brother waking so sweaty
each morning they cut the plastic feet out of
his zip-up pajamas, his damp toes leaving
animal tracks along the hall, my father
honking his horn at anyone going too fast
or slow on the road or failing to flick on
their turn light, my mother always begging
no middle finger at the treacherous curve,
any nut can walk right out of a shop with a gun,
my grandfather quietly bawling when the strand
of far-off pines at the edge of the south pasture
browned and spindled, *his praying place*, grandma
informed us wiping her hands on faded apron
ducks, *the only place he ever felt like God liked him.*

It's as if none of them ever got the letter about
it being a difficult country, the faucet's drip-drip
-drip steadily taking away what small fortunes we
may have hoarded in fatter times, my Uncle trying
to crawl into the casket as the last hymn played,
four deacons to pry him out and sit him back
in the pew, sparse eyed, gulping down glass
after glass of dry air as the piano triumphantly
tinkled towards some far off, rumored victory.

JENN BLAIR

EDWARD MULLINS'S LAST CONFESSION

I despaired when I first understood
the greased, expected word rolling
off my tongue was a lie stinking
up my breast. Does that make
me a traitor? Wanting to get along.
Not having anyone worry or pray
for my lost soul. Everyone else's
head bowed neatly after the sermon
but what discord rattled around inside?
Or was I the sole unquiet. Never
brave enough to ask, I never knew.
How many hours did I spend staring
at the map of Paul's missionary journeys
in the Sunday school room, studying
those indecipherable red tangles of arrow
thinking *shit.* Judge me how you will,
but if faith is a gift, who is the Giver
and how does He portion it out?
What if He wanted to see me wrestle
a scrap (for testing or sport I can't say).
I may have always mumble-mouthed
the hymns, relieved to come to the last
straggle of verse and sit again, but
I've been out in my fields at dusk,
the sun sunk low and red in such a way
anybody would tremble, bow the knee.

Anybody would say *sorry,* would say
thank you, words I bring now one last time,
my widow's mite, my spindle-lamb,
shivering and present on the altar.

JENN BLAIR

MAYDAY

Living all these years with the knowledge, I unintentionally had a small part in trying to tell the world a truth, it, as a whole did not care to hear, and the accompanying criticism makes one feel unnecessary at times.
—Nina Paxton, Ashland, Kentucky, July 22, 1968

You wear thick
serviceable shoes
to walk through
urine starched rooms
where you come to each
bed adjusting the sheets
and your voice accordingly
a cheerful lilt or a hushed tone
dispensing faith or hope
as you can but if someone
asks is it bad and it is
you dare not lie for the
dead know the truth
even more than the sick
such as the man who fell
under the new machine
which spits out steel at the
Armco mill. Some bear up,
the worker at the oil refinery
who lost his left eye to an explosion
telling his weeping daughter
his remaining one was about
to collapse bearing the weight
of so much beauty. Some,
already stressed, buckle,

the woman who broke
her arm and leg and lost
her mother's prized Fox
and Geese wedding quilt
the winter the Ohio flooded
staring up at the ceiling
whispering this isn't my life
this isn't my life as if the saying
would make it so. You try to
meet each where they are
and when the shift is over
you go home and eat dinner
and sit in a soft chair
by the console and all the
bodies, to your relief, turn
to voices, everyone suddenly
light enough to swim
through the waves as
you move your neck
from side to side
rotate your tired shoulders
and listen to the air fill,
then suddenly the hospital's
walls come roaring back,
someone's in distress,
there's been a crash,
a person is injured,
so you scramble for a
pen, you write it down,
there's no time to lose.
You must help at once.

You call, write letters.
Give interviews, year
after year, but no one listens.
The missing aviator?
Someone else would have
heard her too. Someone
else somewhere else
in a different time zone.
You must be mistaken.
Confused. A life so ordinary,
so middle-aged as yours
clearly needed some attention
so you went and invented
the fantastical tale. A woman
asking a woman for help.

JENN BLAIR

FANTASY WORLDS

MONIC DUCTAN

When I was in high school, my favorite actress was Katharine Hepburn. She wore those man-style trousers, and with her neatly coiffed hair she was the perfect mix of tomboy and girly girl. She had the most unusual voice; it was not so pleasing to the ear and very nasal. Kate stood tall and radiated elegance in her films. It's not hard to understand why a teenage girl would admire her, but when I told my momma all of this as we stood in our kitchen, she smirked at me.

"Katharine Hepburn?" Momma asked. "Is that the redheaded one?"

"I don't know. I've only seen her in black and white."

The apples in Momma's cheeks grew more pronounced as she smiled wider. Momma's amusement grew when I told her Kate was someone I'd like to befriend.

"That ole white lady?" Momma laughed. "If she's alive, she's a hundred."

I wanted to be friends with Kate because she was so different from anyone I grew up with in the nineties. No one dressed like those old film stars. No one was so polished, especially not in my family. Momma worked in a poultry processing plant. She came home with her hair in a net, smelling faintly of chicken shit.

I read stories about bold, tomboyish, unpopular Kate. People like her proved it was okay to be eccentric. What I didn't realize as a teenager was that being eccentric when you are a wealthy person is not like being eccentric when you're an ordinary teenager in a working-class, black family. Burying my nose in a book or watching old movies did not qualify me to be admired as Kate Hepburn. For me, being different meant being lonely, which my father was sure to point out. He scrutinized me, and sometimes when he saw me read a book or watch an old movie, he shook his head and said with sadness and pity, "You live in a fantasy world."

He was right. I was lonely, so I made Kate Hepburn my friend by watching her movies. I was poor and lusted after her polished outfits. Daddy was an alcoholic, so I read teenage wish fulfillment books like the *Sweet Valley High* series, in which the characters rarely had serious problems—and those they did have were solved within the space of 140 pages.

Even though Daddy was right about me living in a fantasy world, I still fumed at him for calling me out. I needed to escape his drinking, the thing that pushed me the furthest into my own world. Who was he to shame me for living in it?

■ ■ ■

When he was drunk, Daddy spent his days in my parents' bedroom with the door closed, but when sober he came out and criticized us. He ridiculed my brother for his weight problem and made me feel uncomfortable since he favored me. But he rarely spoke at all when drunk. He usually came home with the liquor in a brown paper sack, bottles clanking together as he walked. When he disappeared into my parents' room and shut the brown, rickety door, we all understood the unspoken rule: Don't bother me; stay away.

My momma's way of avoiding him was to lose herself in soap operas. When she came home from her job at the poultry, she planted herself on the couch in front of the TV and tuned in to *General Hospital*. She didn't like to be bothered when she was on that couch. As a small child, I wanted to read board books and Berenstein Bears with her, and I had to pull her arm and whine to get her attention. She never shooed me away while she watched her soaps, but she wanted to. As I read aloud to Momma, she focused on Frisco, Robert Scorpio, and Anna Devane, three TV characters whose lives were infinitely more exciting than ours. She sat in sock feet, eating a Little Debbie snack cake with a glass of Sprite. Sometimes she peeled open a can of Spam, cut out small chunks of the slimy meat and stuck them between two slices of mayonnaise-slathered white bread. To this day, the mention of Spam—the way it slid in its own juice across my momma's old-fashioned stoneware plates—takes me back to that trailer in north Georgia and the rapt attention Momma paid to *General Hospital.*

While Momma watched soap operas, I escaped from Daddy's alcoholism by reading books, and when the TV was available, I watched those old films. *Bringing Up Baby* with Kate Hepburn and Cary Grant was my favorite. It was comedic genius. *The Philadelphia Story* and *Woman of the Year* entranced me, but my taste in old films wasn't limited to Kate's body of work. In my early teens, I discovered *Gone with the Wind*—the big, hoop skirts, the sweeping music and, of course, Scarlett O'Hara. Her tenacity and gumption were desirable traits.

■ ■ ■

While I immersed myself in fiction, Daddy's health began to decline. One morning during my senior year in high school, he came into my bedroom slurring the words, "I can't talk."

I lay on my bed, propped on one elbow, and watched him as he stood in front of my dresser.

"C-can't talk," he said again.

It sounded like his tongue had been removed or like he had a mouthful of Listerine. For a moment I thought he was choking, but I didn't make a move to help him. I had no concept of what was happening.

Momma, who had followed him down the hallway to my room, came through the doorway. Her eyes darted back and forth between Daddy and me. She asked him to follow her. I don't remember if she drove him to the hospital or if they called an ambulance. I do remember that I went to school as usual that day and every day afterward. I pretended that nothing was wrong, that it was normal for my daddy to be hospitalized.

When I visited him in the hospital, he sat forward in bed and inclined his head toward me. The blue and white hospital gown left his back naked and hung loosely from his body. His movements were jerky. At one point his physical therapist stepped closer to him and said, "Before you make any movement, you have to stop, Mr. Stewart, and train yourself. Don't try to move too much or sit forward until you've gathered yourself, okay?"

She spoke to him as if she were giving instructions to a first grader. Would Daddy have to live the rest of his life this way, confined to a bed and unable to sit forward without running the risk of toppling over? He kept trying to talk to me, but his words were mostly incomprehensible. I couldn't wait to get out of the room.

I wished I had heard her wrong, that the word "stroke" has been somehow carried in through the bus's open windows...

That same week I rode the school bus with my basketball teammates to an away game. My coach asked how Daddy was doing. I was sitting off to myself near the back of the bus. When she asked me that, I wondered who had told her that Daddy was sick. I hadn't said anything to her about it.

"The doctor said a blood vessel burst in his brain," I told her.

The wind, so noisy in my ears, whooshed through the open bus windows.

"So he had a stroke?" she asked.

I wished I had heard her wrong, that the word "stroke" had been somehow carried in through the bus's open windows, and that if I just willed it away it would fly out again. I had heard the word used before in other contexts, and I had grown to think of it as a killer, like cancer and heart attack. I thought the word meant Daddy was going to die.

It was the first time anyone used the word stroke in reference to what had happened with Daddy. Our family never spoke earnestly about his alcoholism and health problems. Growing up in my family, I learned to shut myself off from everyone. I learned to be silent at home and at school, too. I thought that no matter how decent people seemed, they would always disappoint me like my parents. I withdrew into a world of movies and books, partly because inhabiting a fictional world was not as messy as dealing with real people. No matter how many times I watched a Kate Hepburn film, the characters and the ending would always be the same, but in the real world people were unpredictable, my daddy in particular. He sometimes went through periods where he abstained from drinking, and those were followed by his dark periods, during which he drowned everything in liquor.

■ ■ ■

Daddy began to speak and move normally again after weeks of speech and physical therapy. However, there was one skill he never recovered.

"Why don't you read the newspaper anymore, Daddy?" I asked him once.

He sat down at the kitchen table and looked up at me.

"I can't understand it no more," he said. "I can read it, but it don't make sense."

He could comprehend spoken language, so why couldn't he understand written words? I'd always loved books and couldn't imagine how I would feel if I were somehow rendered unable to comprehend them.

Daddy put his palms flat on the table as if he intended to push himself up to stand. As he struggled, I had the feeling that I wasn't watching my daddy anymore. He was someone else entirely. In an old photo on the wall beside the kitchen table, a younger version of him lifted my brother Nathan above his head. In the picture Daddy's arms looked strong and taut, but the man who pushed himself up from the kitchen table in front of me had loose flesh hanging off his arms, which were thin to the point of scrawniness. His narrow face revealed prominent cheekbones.

The man I had been slightly afraid of during had a loud, deep voice, especially when angry, and I always shrank away when he yelled. As I watched him struggle to stand, it was a wonder that his figure had once been so imposing. The 6'1" Daddy of mine who had once weighed 240 pounds was gone.

It hurt to look at him in his weakness. I turned from the table and walked away.

■■■

Daddy's health worsened in the years that followed. He fought stomach cancer and what at least one doctor diagnosed as cirrhosis of the liver. Sometimes he could barely walk because of the fluid in his legs. His heart disease, stroke, liver problems and cancer were all caused by the abuse he put on his own body, and so I blamed him for the drinking and for his habit of chainsmoking. Anger, resentment and worry consumed me.

There is nothing sadder than watching someone die in poverty. I couldn't handle it. I was in college in Atlanta, and even though my parents' trailer in Commerce was just sixty miles from my apartment in DeKalb County, I only went home about twice a year. I managed my full-time job while I sleepwalked through my full-time course load at Georgia State University. When I wasn't working or studying, I holed up in my apartment, half-buried under a pile of books and DVDs, trying to not think about him.

In 2003 at a drugstore in Metro Atlanta, I saw pictures of Kate Hepburn on the cover of a magazine. One of the photos was in color, and I could see that she was indeed a redhead. When I picked up the magazine to look at it more closely, I saw that it read *Katharine Hepburn 1907-2003.*

Something rolled over in my belly. I did not tear up, but I felt as though a friend had died. It was strange to want to mourn her death, not just because I never knew her, but also because I was twenty-one years old and had not watched any of her movies since high school. Even now, fifteen years after her death, and I still haven't been able to watch any of her films. To see them would bring back too many painful memories of my teenage years. How could I watch *Bringing Up Baby* without thinking of the trailer where I first saw it?

I remember a humid night in late springtime, my back slick with sweat, the old box fan whirring in our living room window. Kate picks up the phone and says in her goofy voice, "When you hear the tone, the time will be...When you hear the tone, the time will be..."

Daddy coughs his raspy, smoker's cough in my parents' room.

Toward the end of the movie, Daddy walks through the living room and out the front door as I laugh at Kate's performance. A few minutes later, I peek outside. Daddy stands in front of our old persimmon tree. A cigarette glows bright neon between his fingers. He turns his back to me, not wanting me to see that, despite his mounting health problems, he continues to smoke.

■ ■ ■

In 2005 during my last semester at Georgia State, I got a phone call from my oldest brother Darrell. I had always been a little jealous of him because he was twelve years older than me and all grown up and out of the trailer by the time Daddy got really sick, so he wasn't around to see the worst.

On the phone that day, Darrell told me Daddy had been hospitalized again and that I should come home. He didn't say, you better hurry up, but I heard it in his voice.

I stood on a sidewalk in downtown Atlanta, staring down the sidewalk grate into a dark hole. I told Darrell I'd go back to my apartment and wait for my husband Charlie to come home, that we'd drive to the hospital together that evening.

"Okay," Darrell said, drawing out the second syllable of the word. "Are you sure?" he asked. "I can come now and pick you up."

"No, it's fine. I'll be there a little later, okay?"

I probably should've let my brother pick me up, but I was stalling. I didn't want to go.

When my husband and I got to the hospital, Momma and my brother Nathan were both there with Daddy's sister and one of my uncles.

My heart was in my throat as I entered his room. A tube snaked its way down from Daddy's nose. He fiddled with the little clamp on his finger and winced, as if it pinched his skin.

He looked at me and said, "It's about time you showed up."

I made a whimpering sound but couldn't manage a reply.

His eyes and face softened. "I hate to see my baby cry."

What he said next was completely unexpected: "I love you so much I can't explain it. If there's anything I've done to hurt you, I'm sorry."

Not long after that Daddy began to vomit blood, and the nurse told me to get out of the room while she took care of him.

One of the staff members brought out some forms for Momma to look over. As we sat together in the waiting room, Momma explained to me that when Daddy's heart stopped he didn't want to be resuscitated.

"Are you sure that's what he wants?" I asked her.

"Yeah. He told me. He don't want them to keep him alive like this."

The doctor told us that Daddy's heart was only performing at fifteen percent of what a normal heart should. He was scheduled to start dialysis for his kidneys the following week, but the doctor said there'd be no use since he didn't have a fully-functioning heart.

I felt like my own heart would stop. I hugged my arms around myself so tightly that my fingernails pinched into my skin. I needed comfort. My sullen, reticent parents seldom offered affection, and so as a child I rarely received hugs and I-love-yous. I didn't learn to accept hugs until I grew into adulthood, which is a strange thing to admit. How could a person be unable to accept a hug? All you do is put your arms out and squeeze, right? But it wasn't so simple for me.

I needed people desperately, and on that day when the doctor confirmed my daddy was dying, I especially needed to be hugged.

For a long time, I had the attitude that it was not even worth it to make friends, that being alone was ideal and hugs were unnecessary. Those were all lies I told myself to feel better about not having friends. I needed people desperately, and on that day when the doctor confirmed my daddy was dying, I especially needed to be hugged.

Momma stood right there beside me in the hospital hallway, but I did not hug her. My husband Charlie sat right around the corner in the waiting room, but I didn't go to him either. Charlie had often expressed his frustration that I didn't talk to him enough and I wasn't affectionate. Whenever an emotional crisis arose, regardless of how much I wanted to be comforted, I pushed everyone away.

■ ■ ■

I didn't stay more than twenty-four hours with Daddy. I promised to see him in a couple of days, but when I said it and met his eyes, he looked away. He didn't believe I'd be back.

Two days later when I called my momma and told her I was coming back, she told me she was just leaving the hospital and to meet her at the trailer.

"Are you sure? I can meet you up at the hospital," I said into the phone.

"No, just meet me at home," she said again.

When I got to the trailer, two of Momma's sisters and my cousin Kalisha were already there. We all waited for Momma to come home, and when she finally did arrive she came through the back door and walked slowly across our kitchen toward me. "I'm sorry, baby," she said. "He's gone home."

I didn't respond. I walked from the kitchen and into the bathroom, sat on the floor in one corner and wept. Kalisha came and sat on the lip of the bathtub. She rolled toilet paper from the holder and handed it to me. I blew my nose and wiped my eyes, collecting a small mountain of used tissues in my lap. Kalisha took them from me, accepting the wet tissues without even making a face, filling the wastebasket.

■ ■ ■

Daddy died in February, and I spent that following spring and summer engrossed in books and movies. A thrift store on Lawrenceville Highway sold old paperback books for fifty cents. I was still a *Gone with the Wind* fan, so when I found a copy of the book at the thrift store, I bought it. I expected to love it as much as I'd enjoyed the film adaptation. I lay in bed and read the entire novel in about a week. The book presented the same storyline of the movie I loved so dearly, but in the book Margaret Mitchell's disgusting habit of comparing all of the black characters to animals, mostly apes, was off-putting. I wished Mitchell had been smart enough to think more progressively, to be ahead of her time, to defy the crowd.

Her book romanticizes the antebellum era and sends the message that the perfect, genteel Old South, a land of cotillions and magnolia trees and blacks who knew their place, is "gone with the wind." Mitchell expects readers to be swept away in the romance of it all, which was perfect for me as a child because I so desperately needed romance—the reality of my life was too much to bear.

But as an adult I realized *Gone with the Wind* isn't so romantic. Scarlett's money-grubbing habit of marrying anything rich is not romantic. The way Rhett Butler spoke to her and man-handled her is not romantic either. When he leaves at the end and claims to not give a damn—yeah right, Rhett—you just know he's coming back. But what will happen then? Two obstinate, selfish people cannot build a fruitful marriage.

After I finished reading *Gone with the Wind,* I rented the movie and watched it again. Though I had seen it a dozen times before, it was somehow different when I watched it in my little apartment in Stone Mountain just a few months after Daddy's death. It was like I was seeing it all for the first time.

Picture the scene at Twelve Oaks right before Scarlett sneaks downstairs to see Ashley. All the debutantes are lying across the beds. Young Negro girls fan them with feathers.

Scarlett stands in front of a mirror in that huge hoop skirt of hers and pinches her cheeks to add color to them.

As a child, I watched that scene over and over in our dilapidated trailer, ignoring the scent of my daddy's menthol cigarettes, my body leaning toward the screen. That scene was near-perfect. How lovely and feminine the girls looked in their lacy, white underthings. The music playing in the background reminded me of the tune from the old-fashioned jewelry box I owned; it sounded like a lullaby.

But watching that scene as an adult who was becoming more and more socially and culturally aware, I realized that had I lived in the world of *Gone with the Wind* I'd probably be assigned to hold a feather fan. I didn't think I would fare well as a slave. I would have waved the fan only long enough to coax everyone to sleep, and then I would have slit Scarlett's throat in the middle of the night and taken off north for Canada.

My dissatisfaction with *Gone with the Wind* mirrored my feelings about life in general after Daddy's death. The anger and hurt I'd harbored since childhood just welled to the point that nothing was enjoyable, not even the movies.

Daddy had been right to imply that there is something wrong with living in a fantasy world. To live in such a world does not solve real-world problems or even detract from them. While Kate Hepburn and *Gone with the Wind* helped me survive my childhood, those times could have been better survived had I faced my problems head-on. Watching those movies only made me less lonely for a little while, and they couldn't make up for the time lost between Daddy and me. Rather than focus on movie characters that did not even exist, I should have driven up to Commerce more. I should have made my love more apparent.

Did I love him? If I'm being honest, it was a mixture of love and hate. I hated what he did to his body with the cigarettes and alcohol, and how it affected our family. I hated his propensity for emotional and psychological abuse, his bullying and physical violence. And yet I know I would not have such guilt and regret about not being a better daughter if I had not loved him.

If my life were like most Hollywood movies, I'd have cried and gotten over it all by the final act. But here in the real world I still can't think of him without feeling regret. Sometimes when I'm in that trailer in Commerce, sadness overwhelms me in certain rooms—the bathroom where I sat for an hour and cried on the day he died, the bedroom where he was sometimes laid up with swollen ankles and legs.

He haunts me in other ways, too. Though it's been over ten years since Daddy's death, I can't pass the liquor section of a grocery store without thinking of him. I am sometimes tempted to buy several bottles of wine and liquor and take them home with me. The thing that stops me is that I am afraid of what alcohol could do to me. I have an obsessive personality, and the last thing I need to become obsessed with is alcohol. I am told I look just like him, so I probably inherited more than the looks. I'm sure whatever rotten thing inside of him that caused his dependency is also inside of me.

But I have one advantage over him: I have realized the dangers of living in a world of my own. I'm not sure Daddy had enough self-awareness to know that I wasn't the only one who lived in a fantasy world. His way of escaping our poverty and his own personal failings was to drink whiskey. He'd drink until he passed out, asleep in a fantasy world of his own. ■

PAINTING PAPER AIRPLANES

Reality, a thing to starve and deny,
he held tight faith in his squadrons' design:
the fluting along each fuselage,
the extra crimps of twin tail fins,
the slight down-slope of the noses.
Adding red-white-blue stripes
meant he launched each with a little
more muscle—like jets.

To paint or embellish paper planes
weights them like prayer.
These were not his first, but the first
made distinct, knowing paper's lifespan
yellows faster than vision.

Because youth requires exploration
of each new world, with what tools
and on what vessels we have license,
he mounted the fire lookout tower
high above the city park.

The thin pilot of his imagining climbed
into the blue outline of cockpit.
He soared through the alley of his initiation
into the knife club. Floated over the general
store of his first disguise as thief. Zoomed
past the neighborhood of his future gang's

race wars. Blasted through his backyard
of family fist fights to hang, one last second,
above the church of glossalalia and serpents,
then gide off toward horizon's undulation.

RON HOUCHIN

BOOK REVIEW

Meredith Sue Willis. *Their Houses*. Morgantown, W.Va.: West Virginia University Press, 2018. 252 pages. Softcover. $19.99.

Reviewed by Emily Masters

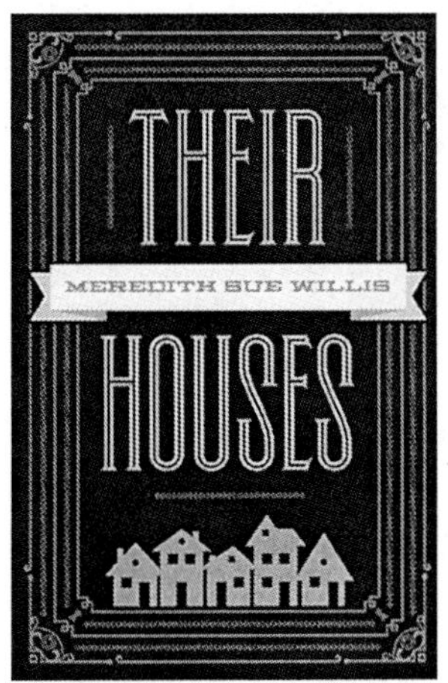

Meredith Sue Willis's new novel, *Their Houses*, focuses on the lives of two sisters (Grace and Dinah) and their childhood friend Richie. Willis, who has authored twenty-two books including *A Space Apart* (1979) and *Love Palace* (2014), here writes an unpredictable, and at times, convoluted, novel about the ways in which the three main characters have found themselves on divergent paths in life, and how they are all pulled back together. The novel features characters who are falling apart, characters who uplift each other, and memories that threaten to topple old bonds.

When Richie discovers he has a chronic illness, he devises a plan to get Dinah and Grace to come back to him so they will all be back in the same place like old times. He moves to the same town where Grace lives with her husband and children. He hooks Dinah's prisoner-turned-priest husband into returning by offering him a job as an airwave preacher, tricking Dinah back into his life without revealing his true identity. With Grace's encouragement, Dinah comes back to live near her and to help her through the depression she is experiencing. Dinah returns to face a world in which she and her husband cannot so fully shield their children from a world lacking in the religiosity they deem so important. Together, Dinah, Grace, Richie, and their families work through issues that have lingered from their childhoods, learning to weave together a tentative community despite their differences.

The characters in *Their Houses* are well-developed and quirky. Grace and Dinah, who grew up in a broken household after their mother suffered from a mental breakdown and their father turned to alcoholism, have chosen opposite paths in life: Grace leads a conventional married mainstream lifestyle, while Dinah is married to a preacher and chooses to shelter her children from an non-Christian world. Their childhood friend, Richie uses his riches to bring the sisters back into his life and is particularly interested in Dinah whom he has always loved. Perhaps the most distinctive character in the novel, however, is Aleda, Dinah's fifteen-year-old daughter who is bucking up against her family's traditional values and wants to strike out on a more progressive path.

Themes in Willis's novel include family, community, religion, friendship, mental illness, sexual assault, and coming of age. Willis toys with the boundaries of family, both blood and bond. Richie desperately wants the kind of family bond he knew from his childhood spent with Dinah and Grace, but

Dinah particularly wants to cut all ties to her rocky past and embrace the future she has found in her religion and with her children. Aleda is biracial and consumed by curiosity about her biological father, but she loves her stepfather, Raymond, as if he is her true father.

Perhaps the most fulfilling aspect about Willis's novel is the way it engages themes of mental and physical illness. Using Grace and her mother, Willis writes about depression and psychosis in an artful way, paying due diligence to the complexity of these illnesses. Dinah and Grace's mother is represented as deeply troubled by the voices in her head, trying to convince her to kill her own children but unable to maintain control of her mental faculties, leading their father to institutionalize her. Their father, unable to cope with his grief at losing the woman he loves to her own mind, turns to alcohol, eventually letting it consume his life, leaving Dinah as the one responsible for herself and Grace. One of the lines from the book that best represents the way the two young girls had to grapple with their parents' illnesses is when Grace reflects, "They always used the proper words, to remind themselves that they were speaking of illnesses: their father was an alcoholic; their mother was psychotic." After suffering from postpartum depression, Grace fears she is turning into her mother, that she will one day share the desire to harm those she loves most. Richie, too, suffers from a physical illness with the Lou Gehrig's disease (ALS) he inherited from his father, which he self-medicates using marijuana.

While Willis's characters are engaging, their relationship and the way they are brought back together is at times confusing and somewhat unbelievable. The fact that Richie creates a compound just to bring back two sisters who he has not seen in years will force readers to suspend disbelief. Raymond, Dinah's preacher husband, is all too quick to jump at the opportunity to work for Richie who employs two of his old convict buddies when he places so much emphasis on how much his life has changed in favor of the Lord. The writing seems almost to border on fantastical at moments like these when almost any other outcome would seem more likely than the one at hand.

Even though there are moments that do not quite ring true in *Their Houses*, the characters themselves certainly do. Through them, Willis provides an artful examination of both physical and mental illnesses, and reveals the struggle that often goes on behind the scene for children who grow up with parents suffering from such conditions. These qualities, coupled with the increased attention being paid to mental illnesses globally, make this novel a timely, relatable read. ■

Jesse Graves & William Wright. *Specter Mountain*. Macon, Ga.: Mercer University Press, 2018. 67 pages. Softcover. $16.00.

Reviewed by James Owens

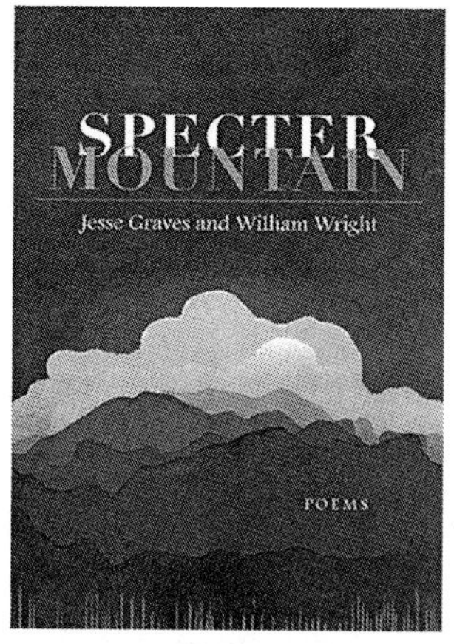

In his poem, "How to be a Poet," Wendell Berry advises, "Stay away from anything / that obscures the place it is in." This is essential wisdom, certainly for a poet, but equally for any person or any group of people, no matter how large or seemingly powerful. A nation or a civilization is a lesser thing than the earth where it has sprung into being, and these make barely a flicker against the background of deep, geological time, though lives lived firmly in place also share something of the eternal. *Specter Mountain*, by Jesse Graves and William Wright, speaks eloquently from inside this truth.

Graves and Wright should be well-known to readers, and to readers of poetry in Appalachia, in particular. Both have already produced rich, necessary work as poets and editors, and now their collaboration is an occasion for gratitude. *Specter Mountain* offers many types of beauty and pleasure, including fine instances of what some of the more thoughtful recent writing on poetics means by "eco-poetry."

The work of any writer associated with a particular place—whether Appalachia or the wider South or any other locale— has taken on a special urgency in recent times, when many places and the ways of life that people have invented to fit them feel the threat of change or extinction. Where resistance to these threats fail, eco-poetry must assume the unhappy work of acknowledgement and grief and warning.

Many people in twenty-first century America live in the midst of things and attitudes and economic structures that, as Berry writes, "obscure" the places they are in, from the largest cities to rural areas left in pain by the disappearance of traditional ways of life with little to replace them except poverty or migration. Specter Mountain chooses not to dwell long on the already familiar consequences of living in these "desecrated places"—Berry's phrase—but when it does offer a portrait of contemporary anomie, the effect is chilling and indelible. In Specter Mountain, this can perhaps be best seen in "The Estranged," which shows us

the truck-bed boys of a silent town,
where violence buds in their hearts
like pulsing nettles, brown calculi

of hard drugs knitted between
their teeth. They smile with a blade's exactness.
Nights they piss in the gardens

of strangers and light cats on fire,
laugh at the pain and yowls.

"This is not a fiction," the poem goes on to insist, "this is hidden / fact, the petrified senses of those / who look away for good"—that is, those who look away from the local facts of life on the mountain, in search of some illusion of "good" in a culture disconnected from the ancient and provident earth. "The Estranged" gives a reader a glimpse into a life, if we want to call it life, that is thankfully not universal in contemporary Appalachia or in other battered parts of the country, but is common enough to be recognizable for anyone who has spent much time in communities ravaged by drugs and unemployment and aimlessness. Specter Mountain is not to be found on a map, but it is still located solidly in the real world.

Though *Specter Mountain* gathers an imposing variety of poetic forms and approaches—elegy and hymn and dream vision, ballad and confessional—its particular virtue as a book, rather than as an accumulation of individually satisfying poems, is in its understanding of scale, the meaning of the particular detail's relationship to its background. Here the experience of any poem's immediate speaker is nested inside a living, contemporary community, which is nested inside the historical process of immigration and ancestral experience of the land—and inside geological processes of formation and destruction, orogeny and the shifting of tectonic plates. The book's first poem, "Prologue," opens with a Genesis-like description of the separation of the Earth and the Moon, and no poem that follows will forget its positioning on the world thus made: "And it was said unto gravity, // *heave a stone / at the barren Earth that a moon will form from it—* // and the worlds survived, fractured into existence."

The physical process of rock heaved up and worn down over millennia, its valleys and subterranean passages, is a constant store of image and metaphor for these poems, a literal grounding for history on the mountain, as it emerges out of time. "Chthonic" is paradigmatic in its understanding of interacting cycles of time, beginning with a dream of the geologic past that seems to unite scientific and mythic accounts of the deep, living underground in gorgeously felt language:

I sometimes fall into visions where the Earth
opens, and far underground, beneath the shallow dead
and the waterline, beneath any trace of life,

the world is undone, aortal and blistering,
glowing and darkening, the Hadean palpitant
center.

For all its importance, this vision of the center of the Earth and of everything's origins is momentary, quickly replaced as "valleys / and rivers lean again into their time-worn complexities," and the poem's speaker is confronted with questions of how to live in time on the human scale, where generations come and go and leave but little or ambiguous traces. The sin-obsessed religion of a deceased grandparent, which might have been an inheritance in earlier days, no longer seems to offer much consolation. "What then is a simple solace?" the speaker asks.

The stand of light
between the trees? Perhaps I love the oaks

no matter where I am—on this mountain,
behind the cabin window, or near the stream
because I cannot endure the vision

of the buried body of my grandfather—a man
I could not love for his constant mantras
about the sinful *and* the end. *His home was nearly pitch black*

even on sunny days, any light a leaking toxin.
The only comfort he found was walking fields
in the pre-dawn halflight, always looking down, down

for arrowheads and bannerstones, quartz drills,
old pipes and bottles, some evidence that he moved
and lived, that others had gone, cast off their mundane

legacies.

Memories or other traces of the preceding generations of human lives passed on the mountain are present throughout the book, from Native Americans, such as Sequoyah, who transposed "earth verse" into the Cherokee syllabary, "a traveling tongue, talking leaves / that could carry a message farther than the wind," ("The Residual Site"), to settlers from Ireland and Germany, who brought with them both European myths and agricultural knowledge to be adapted to the steep forests of Appalachia. Those earlier generations lived their lives wisely, if sparely, on the mountain's terms, adapting themselves to the rhythmic cycles of the natural world, imagined in such poems as "Field Tender's Hymnal," whose

German-immigrant speaker foresees continuity for the family he has established on the mountain, planning to pass his land on to his children: "This ground we tend will belong to them, / so I teach what they are ready to learn, / how to furrow the fields without run-off, / to watch the moon for signs to plant."

But the poems are aware that such cultural wisdom faces attrition in more recent times. Though these lines from "The Residual Site" are thinking most directly about the fading of the Cherokee language, we might read them in the wider context of other loses that happen as the young move away, or simply lose interest and connection with the land:

> *Ground water can sing its cold song forever,*
> *but human codes go quiet after fading out,*
>
> *after losing pitch to the ears of the young,*
> *leaving a whole turn of mind, way of being,*
>
> *with no voice in the world, no way to reveal*
> *its secret truth.*

And though the poem ends by reminding us that "The mountain speaks for itself," both preceding and surviving human language and custom, it may be that few people are listening, anymore, and too many of those who live within range of the mountain's voice find themselves isolated and wounded.

There remains beauty and goodness to be found on Specter Mountain, though the title of "Overburden"—meaning the life-bearing layers of soil and stone that are blasted and bulldozed away during mountaintop removal mining operations—suggests that threat is never far distant. Still, "for now, the mountain is whole. For now / the galax and foamflower bloom beyond / themselves." The phrase "for now," repeated throughout the poem, serves as a reminder of the precariousness of ecological health that could be overturned by a single industrial decision, but with each iteration it also builds incantatory force, becoming a spell, praying that life here continue as it is.

These hills burn within
the cosmos, their deep land and the flesh it contains
filled with dimming lamps of stars. For now,
the valley's creel washes up in aster.

Wild dogs sulk under shards
of dusk the limbs reshape nightly.
Mountain lions satisfy their bloody motions.
For now the mountain is whole.

Graves and Wright are poets of serious accomplishment, and these poems sing and play and work as deeply into a reader as rain shaping its passages into the granite heart of the mountain. In doing so, they also shape our attention to matters of importance and our affections to the ways that human life has been lived in our places on earth and the ways that it might, if we try with the right devotion, continue. ■

CONTRIBUTORS

Maggie Anderson has published five poetry collections: *Cold Comfort, The Great Horned Owl, A Space Filled with Moving, Years that Answer,* and *Windfall.* She co-edited *A Gathering of Poets* with Alex Gidzen and edited and wrote the introduction to Louise McNeill's *Hill Daughter: New and Selected Poems,* which significantly helped to revitalize McNeill's work for future generations. Anderson currently lives and works in West Virginia. Her poem "Kissing the Ripe Tomatoes" originally appeared in the Summer 1987 issue of *Appalachian Heritage.*

Born in Knoxville, Tennessee, in 1936, **Marilou Awiakta** is a seventh-generation Appalachian native and self-described Cherokee-Appalachian poet, storyteller, and essayist. Her books include *Abiding Appalachia: Where Mountain and Atom Meet* (1978), *Rising Fawn and the Fire Mystery* (1983), and *Selu: Seeking the Corn-Mother's Wisdom* (1994). Her work has been chronicled in magazines, literary journals, and various anthologies of literature around the world. Her poem "Dying Back" originally appeared in the Spring/Summer 1988 issue of *Appalachian Heritage.*

Jenn Blair's book *Malcontent* is out from Press Americana (2017). Her work has been published in *Copper Nickel, The South Carolina Review, Cold Mountain Review, James Dickey Review, New South, Pembroke* magazine and *The Chattahoochee Review,* among others. She lives in Winterville, Georgia and teaches at the University of Georgia.

doris diosa davenport is a writer, educator, literary and performance poet, and non-traditional scholar who was born and raised in Northeast Georgia, her lifelong inspiration, obsession, and joy. At seventy, she is a lesbian-feminist-bi-amorous visionary working against all the *isms*. She holds a B.A. from Paine College, an MA from SUNY Buffalo, and a Ph.D from the University of Southern California. davenport has published eleven books of poetry, most recently *rectify my soul.* Her poem "hog killing time" originally appeared in the Summer 2005 issue of *Appalachian Heritage.*

Kelly A. Dorgan's nonfiction work has appeared in books like *Performing Motherhood*, research journals like *Journal of Appalachian Studies*, and online publications like *NYMBM*. Raised in Southern Appalachia, she has rooted herself in the mountains where she is an educator and passionate writer and researcher of the intersection of gender, culture, and illness/wellness.

Monic Ductan holds an MFA from Georgia College and has also studied fiction writing at University of Georgia and the Sewanee Writers' Conference. Her work has appeared or is forthcoming in *Still: The Journal, Shenandoah, Water~Stone Review, Tahoma Literary Review, Cold Mountain Review*, and *So to Speak*. Ductan is the winner of both the 2015 Blue Lyra Review Short-ish Poetry Prize and the 2016 Garth Avant Fiction Award.

Brandie Gray is a third-year MFA candidate at Virginia Commonwealth University where she currently serves as the lead associate editor emerita of *Blackbird*. She is a featured *Blackbird* editor in an online interview with *The Review Review*, and a recipient of the 2018 Sewanee Writers' Conference MFA scholarship in poetry. Gray earned a BA in English and creative writing with a minor in communication studies from Hollins University in Roanoke, Virginia.

Richard Hague's prose has appeared in his collections *Milltown Natural: Essays & Stories From a Life*; *Learning How: Stories, Yarns, & Tales*; and *Lives of the Poem: Community & Connection in a Writing Life*, as well as in *Creative Nonfiction, Appalachian Journal, Now & Then, Pine Mountain Sand & Gravel*, and several anthologies. He received the 2012 Weatherford Award in Poetry. He lives, writes, and operates a small urban farm in Cincinnati. His poem "Luna Moth" originally appeared in the Fall 1990 issue of *Appalachian Heritage*.

Marc Harshman is the author of *Fallingwater* (co-written with Anna Smucker), his fourteenth children's book. His most recent poetry collection, *Believe What You Can*, was published in 2016 and won the Weatherford Award in Poetry from the Appalachian Studies Association. His periodical publications include *The Georgia Review, The Progressive, Roanoke Review, Bayou*, and *Shenandoah*. Harshman is the poet laureate of West Virginia and lives in Wheeling.

A native of upper East Tennessee, **Jane Hicks** is an award-winning poet and quilter. She is the author of two poetry collections: *Blood and Bone Remember* and *Driving with the Dead.* Her poetry has appeared in journals and numerous anthologies, and her "literary quilts" illustrate the works of playwright Jo Carson and novelists Sharyn McCrumb and Silas House. Her poem "Paradise Regained" originally appeared in the Fall 2002 issue of *Appalachian Heritage.*

Julia Hogan lives and works in Spartanburg, South Carolina. Her stories and essays have been published or are forthcoming from the *Sonora Review, McSweeney's,* and *december* magazine, among others. Her work was the recipient of the 2017 Student Fiction Award from the South Carolina Academy of Authors. She holds a day job as a victim advocate and volunteer coordinator at SAFE Homes Rape Crisis Coalition.

Ron Houchin is the author of the acclaimed poetry collection *The Man Who Saws Us in Half,* winner of the 2013 Weatherford Award in Poetry, as well as six other collections. His most recent is *Planet of the Best Love Songs.* A retired public high school teacher, he lives on the banks of the Ohio River across from Huntington, West Virginia, where he grew up.

Jeff Mann's poetry, fiction, and essays have appeared in many publications, including *Prairie Schooner, Shenandoah, Laurel Review* and *The Gay and Lesbian Review Worldwide.* He has published three award-winning poetry chapbooks, two full-length books of poetry, a collection of personal essays, a book of combined poetry and memoir, and a short fiction volume, *A History of Barbed Wire,* which won a Lambda Literary Award. He teaches creative writing at Virginia Tech in Blacksburg, Virginia. His poem "Yellow-Eye Beans" originally appeared in the Summer 2011 issue of *Appalachian Heritage.*

Maurice Manning's most recent poetry collections are *One Man's Dark* and *The Gone and the Going Away.* A former Guggenheim fellow, Manning has been a finalist for the Pulitzer Prize and is a member of The Fellowship of Southern Writers. He teaches at Transylvania University and in the MFA Program for Writers at Warren Wilson College. His poem "Reading a Book in the Woods" originally appeared in the Winter 2014 issue of *Appalachian Heritage.*

Jeff Daniel Marion has published nine volumes of poetry, including *Ebbing & Flowing Springs: New and Selected Poems and Prose, 1976–2001*, winner of the 2003 Independent Publisher Award in Poetry and the 2003 Appalachian Book of the Year, and *Letters to the Dead: A Memoir*. His poems and fiction have appeared in more than sixty journals and anthologies, and he has received the James Still Award from the Fellowship of Southern Writers. His poem "The Man Who Loved Hummingbirds" originally appeared in the Spring 1989 issue of *Appalachian Heritage*.

Emily Masters is a senior English major at Berea College where she works as a teaching assistant for Silas House and as a student editor for *Appalachian Heritage* and *Apollon* e-journal. She is from Monteagle, Tennessee, where she lives on a farm with her family. Her work has been published in *The Pikeville Review*.

Llewellyn McKernan is a poet and teacher who has lived and worked in West Virginia for so long she considers it home. She has a Masters in Creative Writing from Brown University and has been an adjunct English professor at Marshall University, St. Mary's College, and the University of Arkansas. Her published works include six poetry books for adults and several poetry books for children. Her poem "Stream" originally appeared in the Fall 1986 issue of *Appalachian Heritage*.

Irene McKinney was the author of seven books and served as Poet Laureate of West Virginia from 1994 until her death in 2012. She served as a professor at West Virginia Wesleyan College, where she founded an innovative low-residency MFA in Writing program. Her poem "Dark Rain" originally appeared in the Winter 2003 issue of *Appalachian Heritage*.

During her lifetime, **Louise McNeill** published several books of poetry, short stories and essays. She was named poet laureate of West Virginia in 1979, and in 1988 she was awarded the Appalachian Gold Medallion by the University of Charleston. Her poem "The Three Ferns" originally appeared in the Spring/Summer 1988 issue of *Appalachian Heritage*.

Rick Mulkey is the author of five books and chapbooks including, *Ravenous: New & Selected Poems, Toward Any Darkness, Bluefield Breakdown,* and *Before the Age of Reason*. Previous work has appeared in *The Georgia Review, Poet Lore, Shenandoah, The Literary Review,*

Connecticut Review, Poetry East, and T*he Southern Poetry Anthology: Volumes I and III.* Mulkey currently directs and teaches in the low-residency MFA program at Converse College.

James Owens's most recent collection of poems is *Mortalia.* His poems and translations appear widely in literary journals, including recent or upcoming publications in *Waxwing, Adirondack Review, Tule Review, The Honest Ulsterman*, and *Southword.* Originally from southwest Virginia, he earned an MFA at the University of Alabama and lives in a small town in northern Ontario.

Elaine Fowler Palencia, now of Champaign, Illinois, grew up in Morehead, Kentucky. She is the author of two poetry chapbooks and two collections of Appalachian short stories, *Small Caucasian Woman* and *Brier Country.* She is now at work on *My Dear Companion: The Civil War Letters of John M. Douthit.* Her poem "The Caryatids of Appalachia" originally appeared in the Spring 2002 issue of *Appalachian Heritage.*

Ron Rash is the author of the acclaimed works of fiction *One Foot in Eden, Saints at the River, Burning Bright, The Cove,* and most recently, *Something Rich and Strange* and *The Risen.* He was named Finalist for the 2007 and 2009 PEN/Faulkner Awards and has won the O. Henry Prize, the James Still Award from the Fellowship of Southern Writers, and the Weatherford Award. His poem "My Cousin Digs My Father's Grave" originally appeared in the Fall 1989 issue of *Appalachian Heritage.*

Gary Thomas Smith is a writer from Eastern Kentucky. His work has appeared in *Still: The Journal, Stirring: A Literary Collection, Inscape*, and *The Pikeville Review,* among other places. He earned his MA in English from Ohio University and his MFA in fiction from the University of Kentucky.

Albert Stewart was the founder of the Appalachian Writers' Workshop and *Appalachian Heritage* magazine. He published two poetry collections, *The Untoward Hills* (1962) and *The Holy Season* (1984), and died in Knott County on April 1, 2001. His poem "Cumberland Waters" originally appeared in the Winter/Spring 1982 issue of *Appalachian Heritage.*

James Still was the author of several works of fiction and poetry, including *The Wolfpen Poems; From the Mountain, From the Valley;* and *River of Earth,* a novel widely regarded as his masterpiece. His final book, a manuscript titled *Chinaberry,* was edited by Silas House and published after Still's death. He died April 28, 2001. His poem "Mine is a Wide Estate" originally appeared in the Spring 1997 issue of *Appalachian Heritage.*

Crystal Wilkinson is the author of *The Birds of Opulence,* winner of the 2016 Ernest J. Gaines Award for Literary Excellence, the 2017 Judy Gaines Young Book Award from Transylvania University, and the 2016 Weatherford Award for Fiction; and the story collections *Blackberries, Blackberries* and *Water Street.* She teaches at the University of Kentucky. Her poem "Terrain" originally appeared in the Summer 2008 issue of *Appalachian Heritage.*

Annie Woodford is originally from Henry County, Virginia. A graduate of Hollins College's MA program in Creative Writing, her work has appeared in *Shenandoah, The Normal School, The Southern Review, Rattle, Roanoke Review, Appalachian Heritage, Still: The Journal,* and other publications. Her poem "Blue Tick Mongrel, Pacing the Pittsylvania County Line" originally appeared in the Fall 2014 issue of *Appalachian Heritage.*